The Perfect Plan

The Secret Formula Behind What The World's Top Performers Do Differently

Donald W. Barden

The Perfect Plan

Printed by:
90-Minute Books
302 Martinique Drive
Winter Haven, FL 33884
www.90minutebooks.com

Cover art by Madison Brown. interior images by Brandon Wattenbarger

Published in the United States of America

160104-00294.3

ISBN-13: 978-0692657799
ISBN-10: 0692657797

For more information on 90-Minute Books including finding out how you can publish your own book, visit
www.90minutebooks.com or call (863) 318-0464

Here's What's Inside…

To Lisa and the Boys

Special Thanks to Indiana, Kansas and Canada, and In Honor of the Greatest Woman I Have Ever Known

The Elite 1% (noun) e·lite one per·cent
[ih-leet wuhn per-sent]

1. (Often used with a plural verb) The choice of the best of anything considered collectively, as of a group or class of persons.

2. (Used with a plural verb) The best-of-the-best persons of the highest class: Only the elite were there.

3. A tip of the classical organizational bell curve, the pinnacle of an organization's performers.

4. An individual or group of persons that is so good, others begin to ask, "Why?"

5. Those typically ignored by management because there seems to be no reasonable explanation for their excellence.

6. Those who have a plan.

7. Those who change their world.

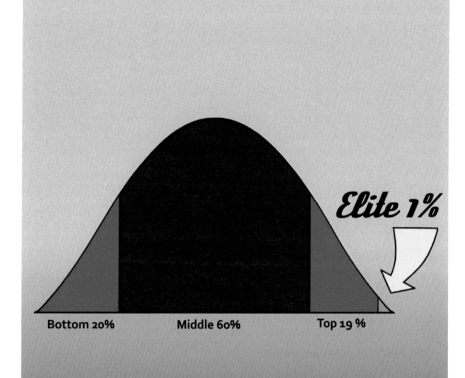

Bottom 20%   Middle 60%   Top 19 %   Elite 1%

What others are saying about *The Perfect Plan:*

"In my 14 years of operating The Brain Trust, we have now seen over 150 speakers. Don's presentation on The Perfect Plan was easily in our top three presentations of all time.

The Perfect Plan is the highest value I have ever seen related to the field of best practices in selling. As a matter of fact, one of our members commented after the presentation that this was more than about selling … it was really about leadership at the highest level."

Tom Cramer – CEO
The Brain Trust

"Don came in to our school and spoke to the leaders and teachers about The Perfect Plan. We were all blown away with what we learned in just a single day."

Trey Arnett
Development Chair and Head of Middle School
Mount Pisgah Christian School

"There is a reason why we see $1 billion in sales, and The Perfect Plan is it!"

James Gilligan
Senior Sales and Marketing Director
OneAmerica Financial Partners

"I have known Don Barden for over 15 years. He has never failed to deliver on any of his commitments. It is rare when you can say this about anyone in today's markets. He is someone I trust and always does the right, moral, and ethical thing for me and those he serves.

Don throws himself passionately into everything he does. Whether it is his family, his faith, his business, or even his health, Don gives 100% effort to achieve maximum outcomes. I admire and respect him both personally and professionally, and have learned many valuable lessons from him throughout the years.

The Perfect Plan is an example of the thoughtful focus he is capable of creating and communicating that hits home with all audiences. Whether you are in the financial industry or not, everyone can benefit from the lessons learned from The Perfect Plan."

James "J" Laschinger
Senior Vice President
Alliant Retirement Services

"After 10 years of fear-based marketing, the clarity on the mechanics of human communication in The Perfect Plan turned my personal and professional communications upside down. The result is an approach that is as calming for someone who hates 'hunting' as it is for my prospects and my family. They now all receive a message of gratitude, key information, and ease of doing business. I look forward to years of rewarding professional relationships … and a happy wife and kid!"

Michael Case Smith
Retirement Plan Advisor
Jacksonville, Florida

"Thank you for The Perfect Plan training over the years. It's changed the way we interact with the world!"

Chris Burr
Financial Advisor – Delray Beach
APA

"I have just gotten back to my desk because of the number of people that have stopped me to declare Don's impact on their life today, and have asked when he can come back and share more of the story. Don has many very special gifts and God is working miracles in and through these gifts. Thank you for sharing the 'Perfect Plan' with our team today. Wow!"

David Mann, President
Strong Rock Christian School

"The Perfect Plan is the missing piece of the puzzle. The Perfect Plan has allowed us into a different context by revealing the act of 'corporate generosity' from organizations offering retirement plans to their employees. It has helped us work closer with plan participants to redefine their retirement in a much more meaningful and achievable way.

As a practitioner managing dozens of retirement plans, having more meaningful conversations with plan sponsors and their participants is everything. The Perfect Plan has allowed us to connect with our clients and prospects at a different level, which in turn has made a tremendous impact to our business and the clients we serve. Thank you, Don!"

Alvaro A. Galvis, CFM, CRPC(r), CRPS(r)
Vice President
Wealth Management Advisor
International Financial Advisor
The MG Group

Introduction

The Perfect Plan started out as a unique idea, a hypothesis that rattled around my brain through the late hours of a warm summer night.

It began on the beach at Amelia Island with 4th of July fireworks. I scribbled on napkins and loose scraps of paper, anything I could find as I watched my children play in the sand.

It was a theory that made complete sense to me, and when written out, it looked even more intriguing. At first, it was one of those ideas that seemed too good to be true, but something inside my head told me it was real.

It felt good because the idea was immensely radical, yet brilliantly simple. As I dug deeper into the concept, I was compelled to question if it could work in real life. Could it live up to the full potential that seemed so obvious to me?

If it worked in actual practice, to what lengths could it go? The impending effect was huge. It was a once-in-a-lifetime, global impact type of concept.

Then I wondered if I had stumbled upon something new and innovative. Or was it an age-old secret? My immediate reaction was naive.

It seemed odd that I had never stumbled upon this it before, yet the simplicity of the Plan made me wonder. It seemed like something anyone with commitment, focus, ethics, and character could achieve.

So, I set out to prove my hypothesis true because, ultimately, I knew that was all that mattered. A theory on paper is intriguing, but it is worthless if never proven. So, from there, the questions became obvious. If it is it true, can it be replicated? That is where the real impact lies, and that was the secret to it all.

So, for the next 10 years, I worked with a team of brilliant men and women to discover if the Perfect Plan was actually "perfect" or not. In the end, we were thrilled with our discovery.

The one thing that stood out to us almost immediately was that the initial idea, the concept, the theory was true — it was the secret practice of the Elite 1% of the world's leaders, sales and marketing teams. It was they who consistently defied all traditional standards of marketing, economics, behavioral strategy, and business logic, and they who became the elite in their fields.

It was there, and in the end, we found the beginning.

We discovered the Perfect Plan.

Chapter 1 – The Unfair Advantage

All anyone wants in life is an advantage.

To be precise, all anyone wants in life is an *unfair* advantage.

Soon, we discovered that the key to the Perfect Plan was unfair. At least that's how some of the lesser informed people took it.

Simply put, the Perfect Plan is the secret formula of the world's most elite leaders, sales and marketing professionals. It doesn't matter who they were leading or what they are selling … the Perfect Plan was there with all of them. From products to policy, from self-esteem to relationships, everyone is selling something, and the Perfect Plan is the key to the elite level of success. Fortunately, we discovered its source, studied its impact, reverse engineered its design, and with critical and controlled trials, proved it to be true. It was the key to the success we all knew was there, but now it became real.

As I mentioned, it all began on July 4th, 2000. That was a great day for everyone. America was celebrating its 224th birthday, the sun was shining on the beach, and the world hadn't ended earlier that year with the dreaded Y2K predictions. It was that day on the beach that I had sunk deep into thought and the idea presented itself to me.

That's where it all began. It was the point where the original hypothesis for the Perfect Plan found its wind. It was one of those moments when your mind is somewhere your body is not, and in that mystic moment, the idea appeared. It was so strong and clear that I immediately knew it was true. I also knew that proving it would be difficult but totally possible. Looking back on that day, I would never have guessed where the path to proving it would take me or how many incredible people I would come to meet. It became a journey that led me around the world to work with and befriend some of the greatest people on earth.

It was a beautiful evening on the beach, where the kids were preparing to shoot fireworks. Our family has made Amelia Island our 4th of July tradition, and I still look forward to it every year. Thousands of people line the beach at sunset, where you can see and feel the fireworks for miles on end. The beach becomes a dreamland of lights that draws you in and envelops you with bursts of colors reflecting off the ocean surf. You can see the fireworks from Georgia all the way to down to Jacksonville and Ponte Vedra.

The fireworks on Amelia Island are "participatory," which means you become part of the show. Not only do you shoot your own fireworks, but they seem to burst around you in a dream-like state, and that lends to an even more patriotic atmosphere. It is always special, and it takes you back to a time and place when America was a little more "real."

I watched the children play on the beach and enjoyed the feeling of living inside the fireworks. That is when I realized something different was happening. I was full of special memories and typical thoughts of 4th of July sentiments when my mind began to drift someplace different. I soon lost my current sense and began to hear a conversation brewing in my head. For the strangest reason, I was not able to shake it. My mind seemed to fixate on the thought but quickly drifted to a consciousness of wonderment. It was a silly feeling at first, but I began to rationalize the thought into a question of "what if?"

So, there it was … a seemingly perfect idea, a working hypothesis, but what if it was true? What was next?

It was one of those moments when I felt like jumping up and down, but my family was there, including my three boys, my wife Lisa, her sister, half a dozen of my nieces and nephews, plus whoever else had wandered over that night. So, jumping up and down like a giddy schoolgirl did not seem to be the best action if people were to take me seriously.

So, later that night after everyone had settled in for the evening, I began to write it all down. I was accustomed to writing late at night, because I had just finished my master's degree and was well entrenched in my doctoral work. Since I had three small children and a full-time career, I rarely began my academic studies until long after sundown, so staying up late with a laptop was nothing unusual. My wife likes to say that I am the only person she ever met who wrote such deep and profound work (she was being a bit facetious) while wearing an old pair of SpongeBob SquarePants PJs — a Father's Day gift my boys had given me a few years before. I was working on my Ph.D. and studying the effects of immigration on long-term pension liabilities absorbed in Europe and the United Kingdom. Exciting stuff, eh? I didn't think so either. Still, it set the stage for what was to come.

As far as academics go, I had just about learned all there was regarding economics and finance. I started moving away from the

2

traditional core curricula and began to go deep into the minds of human behavior. I had reached a place where the academics of economics became frail and the logic a bit weathered. I was becoming bored with the concept of sterile financial decisions and processes.

I quickly came to believe that economics, finance, and even accounting were just historical truths built on records of the past. The numbers that economists used were rarely viewed with any credible forethought concerning the future and certainly never joined itself to any real risk. That's where the Harry Truman joke originated. He once stated that all he wanted was a "one-handed economist" because all his economic advisors kept referring to their "two hands." President Truman complained that everything they told him went something like this:

"Well, Mr. President, on one hand, it could be this, and on the other hand, it could be something completely different."

It was a classical economic explanation — always claiming the only way to know the future was to understand the steps of the past and historical situations that lead them there. They would then toss out disclaimers regarding other possible outcomes, admitting, albeit reluctantly, that human nature has a penchant for changing the direction of its own future.

It is a subtle admission that they, the traditional economists, really don't have very much understanding of the things to come, but they know a ton about the past. To their credit, most economists do acknowledge one significant truth: We (humanity) are all free thinkers, and at any time, we might just forget where we have been and wander off to create a new and unpredictable path. That's the point where I became bored and started looking for a deeper understanding of humanity through the combined study of economics and human behavior. I wanted something beyond the boundaries of Wall Street, stocks, bonds, pensions and, above all, traditional economists.

However you look at it, I was getting bored and was beginning to look for something deeper. That's why that night on the beach came to mean so much to me. When the original hypothesis came, it was more than a new idea; it was a key to unlocking the next step in academic evolution and the start of something wonderful.

Earlier that year, I was asked to write a paper about the person I felt was the world's leading CEO. It was an opinion paper only, not meant to create any traction or distraction. Nevertheless, it planted some purposeful seeds in my mind. So, there on the beach on the 4th of July, I found it strange when that particular paper came rushing back to the forefront of my mind. Suddenly, it all became clear. There was a reason, and there are no coincidences.

The idea I penned that night was an account of what I was convinced to be true. Originally, I wrote it as a fictional narrative because I knew people wouldn't believe it until it had been proven. I hoped that as a metaphorical tale, it might stand a chance of gaining traction and recognition. I know that's not the best way to impact a marketplace, but I wanted to tell the world as soon as possible, even if it meant releasing it before I proved it to be true. It seemed like the best way at the time, and that's where all the logical thoughts in my head were pointing me. Eventually, however, I realized that it was best to wait and follow the protocols necessary for scientific proof. I had a legitimate hypothesis and the ability to prove it, so that is what I needed to do. Fortunately, the days, weeks and years ahead would lend themselves to the proof, and in the end, I was able to answer the question of its validity with 100% confidence.

Yes, the Perfect Plan was true.

What began as a question in my subconscious quickly developed into something special from the very beginning. As the Perfect Plan was revealed to my understanding, I took a deep breath and exhaled. I knew it was good, but I wanted to test and retest it until there was no doubt in anyone's mind.

What we discovered was the method and formula to a practice that would ultimately take me and my team over a 5,000-year journey of research and study as we proved its validity. From Eastern Europe to Mexico, from the United States to India, to Indiana, Kansas and Canada, we checked and rechecked until there was nothing more to prove.

We stripped out the nuances of culture, aligned it through history, and used a variety of comparative analyses, of which no one could have imagined in the beginning. We also came to self-inject the study, as most mad scientists ultimately do, and found that it worked just as well on our own group as it did on all others combined.

—

It was true, it was pure, and it really was perfect.

Ten years later when it was finished, our research and testing held a sense of completeness. That is when we began to reflect across the vast scope of what we had learned.

As the Perfect Plan revealed itself, we found that several other lessons existed and were woven into the fabric of the Plan. These lessons were the fiber that allowed success to come, but unlike the final product, they could each stand alone within their own merits, totally independent of each other. They were principles of success that on the surface seemed easy to understand but were often lost in the shadows of a busy life. There was probably a time in each of our lives when these values had been taught and we understood them, but as we grew and matured, they became lost in our ambitions and desires. Everyone hears them spoken as a child. These principles have been part of our lives since the earliest of days. Those whom we studied never forgot those core lessons, and they gave us permission to open our minds and invite them back.

As my team sat together, we looked across the room and smiled. That is when we began to put the puzzle pieces together. The simplicity of the principles that were woven into the Perfect Plan was astonishing, but it quickly became clear to us that it was not necessarily the ingredients that made the Plan so special.

It was the order in which they built upon each other that propelled the Plan forward.

It was the purity of those organized sequences that opened our minds and touched our hearts to the power it held.

As you begin to explore the truths of the Perfect Plan with me, we will witness what they can do, and in the end, you will find the beginning.

It will be the start of something so perfect that you will be amazed at the future you discover for yourself and the Plan that lies before you.

But what would you do if the entire world were before you?

What would you do with the Perfect Plan?

What would you do once you discover the formula that unlocks the mystery as to why the Top 1% of people throughout history have been so successful at what they do?

What happens when you discover a group of people whose performance is so great that they are literally off any measurable chart?

What happens when seemingly every effort to track their success is for naught, because outsiders get so caught up in the results that they forget to ask "how?" or "why?"

The Perfect Plan is the guide to why the Top 1% of the world's leaders, sales, marketing, political, religious, and business people become successful. It is the one thing that makes the best better than anyone else. The Perfect Plan transcends itself to impact relationships, marriages, family and children. The Perfect Plan lays the steps to success with a foundation so strong that, when sincerely applied and executed, the "close" rate is close to 95%. It pushes all perceived boundaries by allowing an uncontained growth rate in excess of 300% per year! Even better, when properly applied, people are moved, policies are set, sales are closed, markets are leveraged, and great people become leaders.

It is so simple and powerful that when the original hypothesis was proven true, we wanted to tell the world. It was exciting as we set out to share the secret to anyone who wanted to know, but it was 10 years later before it all began to make sense. It was a single day when all the Perfect Plan's final proof came together in one amazing deal.

Leveraging the Unfair Advantage

$450,000,000.00.

That's a lot of money in anyone's book.

In the world of institutional finance, it is just a day's pay, but you have to earn it first. To do so, you have to leverage the deal, and that takes a lot of work. Months of preparation can go into a single presentation that might only last, on average, 45 minutes. That is how long it takes for committees and leaders to decide how to best to deploy their recourses. This particular deal was exciting because there was a bonus. In addition to the $450 million upfront deposit, another $100 million would be spent with the winner of the contract annually for the next 10 years. That's worth the effort.

I wanted this deal badly, but we knew we were not the only team in the running. I had long grown accustomed to how the Wall Street game works, and my own experiences had taught me that the final decision would come down to a single moment in time. The trick was to predict what would become the deciding factor. What would be the committee's tipping point?

- ❖ Would the committee use a complicated set of variables and complex logarithms to deduce which firm would be most suitable to win, or would it be their gut feeling?

- ❖ Would the leadership team follow a time-tested series of principles that have been passed down from generation to generation, or would a simple pretty smile tip the scales in our favor?

- ❖ Would they decide based on their collective academic and business experience, or would it come down to a beauty contest of those who simply "look" the most deserving?

In the moments leading up to such a presentation, these are the thoughts that usually flash through the minds of the hopefuls. At times, the emotions begin to sound like jackhammers pounding on your skulls and eroding away any confidence. Yet, that's where the best start to prevail, because they know that *if, hope, try, and probably* are not strategies.

Our team was different.

We felt good about our chances because we had an unfair advantage.

We had the Perfect Plan.

All of our training came down to this moment.

It is not from pride or ego that I believed we would win the deal. Far from it. Thanks to our work on the Perfect Plan, we had become the best team in the industry by sticking to the Plan's proven process. Since the discovery of the Perfect Plan, we had led the market for years and broken every record in the books. We managed to win some of the most prestigious and sought-after accounts in the country, so why should this one be any different? For weeks, we had practiced and prepped for this moment. We knew everyone's move before they had thought about it themselves. We were the best-trained, best-educated, and best-prepared team in the country. We were ready.

On this particularly sunny day in Southern California, we were set to make our presentation and land this $450 million deal, but there was one seemingly irritating snag. We had drawn (in a lottery pick) the dreaded position of being the first of the three finalists to present. It was the equivalent to starting a NASCAR race as the last car in line.

As a rule, when the decision is at stake, most large institutional clients will narrow their search to the top three contenders and invite them in for a final presentation. They usually enforce strict rules of engagement and ask you to keep your presentation to 45 minutes, which customarily is followed by an extra 10 minutes of Q&A. The same set of rules applies for everyone and is designed to level the playing field for the finalist.

Most good teams will put in over 80 hours of intense preparation for presentations of this size. In contrast, our team spent over 200 hours on this particular client, including design, creativity, style, R&D, and even a little covert guerilla action. So, while being first to present that day was not the most desirable pole position, it didn't bother us in the least. We were professionals and we had the *unfair advantage* no matter which lot we drew.

Our team spent our final day before the presentation at a luxury five-star hotel in the same city as the client. This is customary for several reasons. First, we needed everyone rested and relaxed within the same time zone as the client, and second, we wanted everyone involved in the presentation to feel good about themselves. We also wanted them to know how much their work meant to our

—

8

organization by offering a little "thank you" to the team before the starting bell rang.

It was a token of our appreciation that worked in a variety of ways. The team members who worked the hardest felt a little gratitude, and being pampered at the resort helped them to mentally prepare for the expectations of the client. We always felt that if we immersed ourselves into someone else's service offering (i.e., a five-star resort), then we would take that attitude of servitude into our presentation.

If we *lived* it, we knew we could *deliver* it.

We certainly wanted the best for the client, and there was nothing wrong with having a little bit of fun for ourselves.

We spent the final afternoon in our prep area, running through mock-ups of the presentation room, the gender mixes, and even seating arrangements for the following day. It was always casual and never scripted, but certainly 100% rehearsed. All the details were discussed, even the most minute action. We decided who should enter the room first and who should target whom with their small talk. We knew everything about the committee members. We knew their life stories, personal styles, and their predictable natures. We accomplished this with CIA-type precision. We even set the ground rules for our dress code and discussed how someone should sit during the presentation. We decided how, and if, the women on our team should carry purses into the meeting, even down to which shoulder they would carry it on. It might sound silly to some, but big decisions are made from the smallest of actions; we wanted it to be perfect, and that is never easy.

As a long-standing tradition, just before we began the last day of practice, I would tell my team the story of how I once saw a woman's career collapse because of something so insignificant that, to this day, she still doesn't know how it happened.

The story went like this:

Twenty years prior, as a younger man finishing up with my undergraduate degree, I began hunting for a "real" job. I was a very poor college kid with one month to go before graduation, but I was perfectly content in my role at the time. Yet in the back of my mind, I knew I needed to move on to something more significant to fulfill my career aspirations. While finishing school, I had the incredibly stupid (and fun) job of chasing shoplifters out of a large — very large, actually — downtown department store. I generally had 50 to 100 yards to catch said culprit, knock them down, and wait for the police to show up (that's where the stupid part kicked in).

So, what do you do in the 30 seconds after you knock down a criminal in the seemingly eternal seconds before the police get there?

Pray!

Yet little did anyone know, there was a huge side benefit to the job that kept me from quitting. I spent the day standing in the woman's cosmetics area located by the store's main front doors — the preferred exit route for most of the petty thieves. So, while attentively keeping an eye out for shoplifters, I got to talk with some beautiful girls who worked in the area, making the time pass quickly and pleasantly.

One day just before I graduated, after a 10-hour day on Peachtree Street with another five hours in class, I got home to my apartment to find a peculiar message on my answering machine. (Yes, this predates voice mail, email, and cell phones). The message was simple. I was to show up at work the next morning in my best suit and tie and be prepared to meet the company's CEO. That's all the message said! So, I rushed to clean my best —and only — suit and ended up staying awake all night with wonderful, but terribly inflated, possibilities floating around in my mind. Would I be made a senior financial trader for the firm, head of new accounts, CFO … what would it be? I was breathless with anticipation.

The next day, I arrived as directed and went straight to the CEO's office. Having never been there before, I was in awe of the mahogany panels, the two secretaries out front, and the CEO's own private waiting room. It was old-school, New York- style retail class at its best. I had no idea why I was there, but I knew it would be great.

After a few moments, an elegant lady, the CEO's personal assistant, came out to meet me with the Senior Vice President of Security in tow. I understood why she was there, and I certainly knew who he was, but I had no idea what he wanted with me. They politely took me back to a lovely private parlor room decked out with its own fireplace — *cool, right?* — and began to explain why I had been called and why that day was the first day I would begin wearing a suit to work for the rest of my life.

I didn't know it at the time, but the CEO, who was actually based in New York City, was contemplating moving corporate offices to Atlanta and was about to spend six months commuting up and down the East Coast to test his idea. The head of security wanted me to be there for him and act as his personal staff aide during the transition. While it was a long way from the CFO job that I was naive enough to dream about — what the heck — I got to drive a new Mercedes and hang out with a guy who knew more about leadership, business and marketing than almost anyone else in the world. I did not realize it at the time, but my education in business and life was about to kick into overdrive.

I was all in and loving it.

Over the next six months we were together, I was in a constant state of gratefulness. I was also truly humbled that he treated me with grace and respect. To him, I was a young, eager kid who just graduated from college and was looking to find my way in the world, and it didn't hurt that I was the same age as his grandsons. He taught me more in those six months than I ever learned in the prior four years of college, or would learn over the next six years of graduate, post-graduate and doctoral studies. This was all great, but there was one particular night in New Orleans that made an impression on me like nothing I had ever seen before.

I had grown to the point where I was put in charge of greeting his guests and handling the introductions of people wanting to meet him. Vendors, managers and even a few famous fashion celebrities would meet me before formally being introduced to the boss. To meet with him was like meeting royalty in the garment business, and he was king.

One of his gracious traditions as a great leader was to take a store's management team out for a huge feast the night before they opened a new location. The team consisted of the store's General Manager, Operations Manager, Human Resource personnel, and of course, all the Floor Managers. It was always festive and something I really enjoyed watching. That night we had rented out a local restaurant, famous for its five-star food and service. It was an old antebellum home that had been converted into an incredible eating establishment on the banks of Mississippi River in New Orleans. We had a great time as he toasted their future success. As we finished for the evening and walked out to our car, he was happier than I had ever seen him. He boasted about the quality of the new team and predicted that their sales numbers would break all the records.

Then it happened.

As we got into our car, he saw something begin to unfold in the parking lot, and he asked me not to drive away. He requested that I position our car so we both could watch what was about to happen. I obeyed.

The Operations Manager from the new store had come out of the restaurant and was approaching her car. Everything seemed safe enough, and she followed the proper procedures for any young, attractive woman walking by herself at night. She opened the door and started her car without incident. What happened next became the worst moment of her corporate career as she started to back her car out of a rather odd parking position.

It was actually more than odd. It was impossible.

She had apparently, in an obvious hurry to avoid being late to the dinner, wedged her car on to the curb between a tree, a large Dumpster, and several other cars. She had parked so precariously that she was beyond any hope of a traditional three-point Y turns needed to exit the space. In fact, she was so pinned in that she made over 25 short maneuvers going forward 12 inches, turning the wheel, inching back 12 inches, turning the wheel the other way, forward, back, forward, back — it seemed to last forever.

Once she finally got clear, there was a short moment of anticipation that she might bottom out as she came off the curb.

She did.

In heroic fashion, sparks flew and metal collided with hard Louisiana concrete as her car smashed down off the curb and onto the street. She drove off with an obvious sense of relief, seemingly thinking nothing of her own efforts. It was just another routine New Orleans parking dilemma solved, but there was a problem. No one had seen it — except us.

While she might have thought nothing of it, the boss thought a lot about it.

As he and I sat in relative silence, watching her drive away under the New Orleans streetlights, the CEO spoke to me with an air of disappointment about a something I never saw coming.

12

"That's a shame," he said softly.

"Yeah," I replied, thinking about the damage to her car.

"I hate to see such a bright young woman ruin her career over something as silly as parking a car," he continued.

I blinked, bewildered. "What do you mean? Was that a company car?" I asked, trying to create an awkward giggle.

"No," he said with a slight sigh.

"The truth here, kid, is simple. How can I ever trust her to run one of my stores, if she can't even park a car the right way?"

I turned around to look at him, shocked at the reality of his words.

"Are you telling me that just because she got herself stuck and had a tough time backing out of a parking space, her career is ruined?"

"That's exactly what I am saying." His tone left no doubt to his seriousness.

"You see, son, it is the little things that count and even the smaller things that make the biggest impressions, but don't worry … she's a sharp girl, and I am sure someone else will hire her."

Wow, and she never even knew it.

I tell this story to all my teams before every meeting. I do this not to rehash a sad moment is someone else's life, but to remind them that it's the little things that can swing a sale, and when $450 million is on the table, we had better get it right.

All the study, R&D, and training would mean nothing if the clients become distracted by something so simple that their decision is based on a vague impression instead of your professional work, skill, or talent.

The reason we focus on the smallest detail is not because it will win the deal, but to eliminate any possible distractions that could lose the deal.

You never want to create a disturbance that takes the client's focus off the real decision and your ability to present your work. Too many deals are lost for all the wrong reasons — usually because someone got distracted about a minor detail that others thought nothing about.

If you don't believe me and don't understand that it's the little things that make all the difference, you had better stop reading right now because you fail to comprehend what the best in the world know and understand. Details rarely win a deal, but they exist to neutralize the environment so that everyone can focus on what is most important. If you remember anything from this book, remember this:

If it looks easy, it's not.

So, almost 20 years after that incident in Louisiana, on that day in Southern California, we were grateful, well-educated, and totally prepared to make it look easy. We knew the stakes, and we were ready to win the deal.

Everything went as scheduled that day, and we had a near flawless delivery. The entrance, the set, the transitions, and the presentation — all were as planned and rehearsed. We were simply on point, and it showed.

After we finished, something wonderful happened. The CEO, in a very uncustomary fashion, stood up and came around the boardroom table to meet me. I stood at attention and displayed all the proper courtesies, thinking I was about to hear a routine close to the meeting and a pleasant "thank you." That's not what happened.

As she came close to me, she put out her hand and with a huge smile said the most beautiful words anyone in sales and marketing can ever hope to hear:

"Congratulations, you win the deal!"

I hesitated in shock for a moment, not fully grasping what she said, but it was true! We had won the deal — all $450 million of it.

It was uncharacteristic and slightly out of protocol to award any deal so soon, especially without hearing the other two bidders who were waiting outside the doors for their turn to present, but she must have been convinced that we were the best.

She noted our professionalism and told us that she felt sorry for the others who were scheduled after us. She even went so far as to ask that we return the following Monday to begin the transition and even offered to take us to a celebration dinner following the next meeting. It was simply the best feeling in the world — a $450 million win.

For a moment, a brief feeling of compassion toward our competitors came over me. I knew they worked hard to get here, but in this case, we knew a few secrets they probably did not.

We all shook hands as we exited, and I told them we were looking forward to seeing them the following week.

Their business consultant, a broker who had connected us with the client, was ecstatic. We quickly planned a celebration drink that evening back at the hotel before I flew home the next morning. The rest of my team said goodbye and headed toward an executive airport where our corporate jet was waiting to take them home. I was thrilled to stay behind one more day to debrief with the broker and enjoy a well-deserved victory cocktail. What a day!

That evening around 6:00 local time, I floated out of my room and rushed to the resort's main restaurant and bar for what I knew would be the best post- victory dinner of the year. The broker was a good friend of mine, and we had referred business to each other for years. I knew his family and two wonderful little girls. Best of all, I knew he would be just as happy for our team as he would be for anyone else. I hurried to the bar, arriving a few moments before he did. I had in hand my traditional victory drink, which I had named "Daddy's Little Helper," a Gentleman Jack on the rocks with a slight splash of cola and a lime. As I took my first wonderful and well-deserved sip, it happened.

I looked up and…

Well, suffice it to say, I'll finish this story later.

What is important here is that the Perfect Plan is not an innovation. It is a time-tested, proven process that anyone can master. It takes a lot of work, and it requires a mind open to learning new things, even when things seem so obvious.

Remember: If it looks easy, it's not.

The Perfect Plan is the ultimate *unfair advantage.*

Chapter 2 – The Perfect Plan

The Perfect Plan is the proven process and the secret behind history's best and brightest. It is the communication path that helped move the markets and revolutionized the world. It is the simple steps to a 95% close ratio and a successful life.

It's perfect by its very existence, best of all, it is really good news.

In effect, the Perfect Plan is the result of a collision that occurs between a system of three *Promises* and three *Beliefs*.

When a presentation is made, it follows two district sequences of *Promises & Beliefs*.

It is the logical order of things, backed with scientific evidence that proves why it is so effective. We also learned that as these sequences and proven processes are implemented, an interesting phenomenon occurs. The buyer, prospect, or those whom you are leading become bonded with the you – the presenter/leader. They then clearly understand what is needed, and become relieved at the ease from which it flows.

Then, as the Perfect Plan lays out the pattern of its proven process, the buyer will ultimately want to know *who* you are.

This is where the **three *Promises*** collide with the **three *Beliefs***. The buyer then feels magnetized to you, understands the value you are offering, and glimpses into your forward state of being. Then and only then can the person make a wise decision because they will then ask of themselves **three *questions***. If these are answered with affirmation, they move forward in their conscious approval.

Decision-makers and individuals need to know if harmony exists between what's right for them personally, professionally, and in their spirit. If all three questions are answered "yes," they have a good decision. Yet this is where it begins, not where it ends.

The Perfect Plan is not a magical formula or even a foregone conclusion. It is an extension of *you and the leader inside.* It is ultimately a belief system that is demonstrated in every word, every action, and every thought you make when presenting yourself, your product, or your desired outcome.

Let's take a look at the Perfect Plan in an outline form before we get into a more in-depth explanation.

The Three Promises

The three promises of the Perfect Plan are rather simple. They are:

1. Gratification
2. Education
3. Ease of Business

In that order! The sequence is essential to the process. These promises are what you offer to the prospect or to those you lead. They are an expression of your authenticity and experience.

The Three Beliefs

When the three promises are presented in precise order, the recipient will then want to know *who* you are and what you believe, i.e. your belief system.

The Belief System for the Perfect Plan is made up of three simple states of being:

1. Create, Don't Compete
2. Exceed Expectations at All Times
3. Never Give Back: Always Give Forward, without any expectations of anything in return.

This is the *who* of *you*. The order of the presentation needs to occur in sequential fashion, knowing that the prospect will ultimately want to know *who* you are and *what* you believe.

The Three Questions

Once they know your three Promises and your Belief System, they will then ask themselves three questions. The answers to these questions will ultimately determine the decision they make. They are:

1. Is this right decision for me personally?
2. Is this right decision for me professionally?
3. Is this right decision for me spiritually (in my conscience)?

One of the revelations from the study was that the Top 1% already knows the answers to these questions before they ever make the presentation to the client or those they lead. They (the Elite 1%) ask these questions on behalf of their client to themselves, because their own belief system requires them to be a *servant,* not a leader.

Servants actually begin the process by asking themselves:

"If I am to serve this person, will it be right for *them* personally, professionally, and in their spirit?

If so, then and only then will I present myself to them with an attitude of gratitude, real education, and ease of business — because that's what servants do.

Then I will be there for them with a creative spirit, not a competitive attitude.

I will exceed their expectations at all times.

I will give forward without any expectation of anything in return ... because that's what servants do."

The Top 1% actually turns the entire concept of leadership and marketing upside down because they are not in the leadership and marketing world at all! They are servants, and that is the secret foundation to build the Perfect Plan upon.

While everyone is trying to figure out how the elite lead so well, sell so much, and draw such a crowd, most people miss the divine truth. They overlook the obvious because they are looking at it upside down. Most people are trying to see the two sides of every coin, not realizing that there are actually *three* sides to every coin and every situation — heads, tails, and "the edge."

With a coin toss, every so often, it actually lands on its side. While most people want to choose heads or tails, the Elite 1% knows there are other possibilities.

There is more than the buyer and the seller.

There is more than a leader and the masses.

There is the servant.

The elite become *who* they are and break all boundaries of leadership and sales because they are humble *servants*.

This attitude, along with their *Promises* and *Beliefs,* is what affords them the magical approach that closes so many sales, leads so many people, and ultimately influences human behavior.

Over the next few chapters, we will discuss in detail each of these concepts and how they not only relate to you, but the effect they have on each surrounding principle in order to drive the Perfect Plan forward.

As with the process itself, we start where others think it ends: in the mind of the prospect.

Once we understand why a person (or a committee) makes the decisions they do, we can serve them.

Chapter 3 – Understanding the Decision-Making Process

To better understand how the elite utilize the Perfect Plan, it is essential to understand how and why people make the decisions they do. Understanding that will help you implement the Perfect Plan in the way it was meant to be used.

In the beginning of our journey, we quickly learned that there are three *good* things everyone needs in their lives to make good decisions. Decisions have untold ramifications on the future that cannot be charted in advance or predicted with any real degree of certainty. Therefore, decision-makers must decide based on certain core principles and innate (gut) feelings. They are as follows:

The Need for Good Advice

The first is *good advice*. I'm talking about the kind your parents and grandparents give you. It's the concepts, ideas, values, and wisdom you absorb as a child and build upon as you grow, learn, and mature. It is the sort of thing that you find important but also something you store away for future use.

When you need it, it is there for you. You may choose to employ the advice or not, keeping it for later, but either way, it is always *good*, and it is of great value.

Without good advice, making decisions is problematic at best.

We all need good advice to make future decisions.

Those who consistently make the best decisions are those who seek out good advice.

The Need for Good Understanding

The second requirement for a good decision- making process is that of *good understanding.*

Understanding is how you process the facts and justify your actions. Good understanding is clean, clear, and learned. It is always the foundation upon which you will ultimately build your leadership skills. Good understanding is the evidence that adds to the reasoning upon which you base all your conclusions.

Getting good advice without proper understanding will skew and alter the results.

Understanding is the knowledge of how to employ the good advice correctly. Without the ability to understand, even good advice could ultimately lead you astray.

The Need for Good News

Finally, and most importantly, is what we need to *hear* the most — *good news.*

Unlike the other two, good news is not something you store up until you need it, and it is not something that you have to figure out or study. It is simply what you want to hear. Good news will allow you to relax when you realize that nothing is required from you, and there is nothing to act upon.

Good news is one of the few things in life that can never be bad, and it is always revealed when you need it most. That is what makes good news the most special of them all.

It was good news to us when we realized what the Perfect Plan was to become a key to others' success. It was nothing to fear — it is simply very good news.

All three of these are essential to the decision- making process. They may take different forms and point in different directions, but these are the core ingredients to good decision-making.

In researching these criteria and putting it to the test, we learned that these three lessons were essential to help us bring *good* news to those we served.

25

The Critical Thinking Process

The science necessary to process and understand the difference between good advice, good understanding, and good news is based on a formula that legal and doctoral students learn on their first day of school in Critical Thinking 101.

Critical Thinking is the "proof" process required to convert a hypothesis into something more tangible and meaningful. It is a progression that is inherent in everyone's being.

The *good news* here is that science has a formula, and it is the foundation used to prove every hypothesis and, ultimately, every human decision.

The process and formula necessary to prove every *hypothesis* via critical thinking is:

Evidence + Reasoning = Conclusion

Let's dig deeper. Pretend you're a world-class trial attorney:

Evidence is equal to the "facts."

Before you believe something to be true enough to feel compelled to act on it, you must first understand the facts.

Science refers to facts as evidence.

"Reasoning" in legal terms, is the "motive," i.e. why did they do it?

Once you fully understand the "facts" (evidence), then you combine it with the "reasoning" (i.e. what your previous experiences have taught you) to form the conclusion.

This is this combination of real-life experiences and the emotions that lead you to believe something is true. When the facts and the reasoning combine, the good understanding should, if properly done, become good news.

Let's look at an example.

When someone makes a statement that needs to be proven in order for someone else to decide which action to take, a good scientist will apply trial testing to prove whether the statement (hypothesis) is true.

Follow the logic.

Let's review the following hypothesis: If I smash my hand with a hammer, it will hurt.

This sounds simple enough, and virtually 100% of the people reading this will agree with the hypothesis, but that's not good enough for science or the critical mind. It must first be proven.

So, how do we prove it? By creating a trial that argues the facts (evidence) before it applies the reasoning (motive/emotions).

The words "trial" and "argue" are important here because it implies logic, not conflict. Just like a "test run" before a race, or a "test trial" before new product is released to the public, it's the process that leads us to the proof.

We tend to associate the word "argue" with conflict or even violent disagreement, but it is really not that at all. It is simply the presentation of facts leading to a conclusion before two opposing thoughts or sides.

This is why you don't *present* your case to the U.S. Supreme Court; you actually *argue* your position before the judges and the opposing counsel.

Once the evidence has been tested and combined with the reasoning, the trial is complete. If accurate and true, the sequence will prevail. The process will transform from "advice" to "understanding," then on to a conclusion, which is almost always "good news."

For our example — hitting you hand with a hammer — let's explore the critical thinking process.

1. <u>Good Advice</u>: "You better not hit your hand with that hammer!"

2. <u>Good Understanding</u>: "You know from experience that hitting your hand with a hammer will hurt like the dickens!"

3. <u>Good News</u>: "Whew! Sure glad I decided not to hit myself with that hammer!"

So exactly how would you create the trial in this case? Well, as silly as it seems, you would place a rather dense volunteer's hand on a table and hit it with a hammer at least 10 times. After each strike, we record the results as the facts or *evidence.*

In this case, it's a safe bet to say our volunteer will experience extreme pain every time the hammer hits his hand. Therefore, the facts, or evidence, show that smashing your hand with a hammer is painful. Sounds crazy and simple enough, but that's just the first step.

Now that we understand the facts or evidence, we need to combine it with the *reasoning* or *emotion.* To do so is easy. We ask ourselves if there are any past circumstances that would cause us to believe that hitting our hands with a hammer will be painful. Again, we will have a 100% affirmative response. Most people, especially your poor test subject, will tell you that they have hit themselves in the hand with a hammer at some point in their lives, or at least witnessed someone doing. So, their reasoning concludes that a repetition of the trial would only result in more pain.

This creates an emotional response that overrides the particulars of any specific memory, wanting to avoid repeating a negative action. It also fuels the future options when someone might want to replicate a positive experience. Either way, your gut feelings and reactions based on your experience will be added to the facts you know, dictating your response.

So, let's look at what happens after the trial. If this sounds a lot like the legal process, it should — both are based on logic.

Evidence + Reasoning = Conclusion

1. Evidence (facts): The hand was smashed 10 times by a hammer and 100% of the responses reported that the action produced pain.

2. Reasoning (emotional response): 100% of the emotional recall and response confirms the belief that it will hurt if your hand is smashed with a hammer. This is based on actual and/or similar past experiences.

3. Conclusion (decision): Based on the facts and the reasoning, the conclusion is that hitting your hand with a hammer is painful. Therefore, don't do it!

The conclusion drives the deciding action. The decision is formed from Good Advice, Good Understanding, and Good News. In the case of the hammer ... just don't do it!

Is this just simple science that is dumbed down to seem unreasonable? Not at all.

There is another part to the question that the Elite 1% of the leadership people knows.

The question now shifts from the *process* of critical thinking to asking how much each *part* of the process weighs on the other. Better yet, does the evidence and reasoning share an equal role, or does one carry more power than the other when a decision must be made?

In science, they should be equal, but in human behavior, they are not.

Therefore, to better understand the decision process of a prospect or client, you need to understand how each is weighted in the mind of the decision-maker, the consumer or the person you want to lead your way.

Behind the Numbers

Science has finally begun to look inward for the first time and question theories and established facts with variables that might seem hard to measure. Interestingly enough, we have only now become brave enough to ask humanity's only impossible question to answer:

What do you not know?

Think about it. It should stump you.

It is impossible to know what is unknown to you. If you knew it, it wouldn't be unknown. However, for what we do know, we can begin to look inward and beyond sterile logic. If science teaches us that a conclusion of a good decision is based on evidence and reasoning, then logic dictates equal order and weighting between the two. This is good in a vacuum of space, but as Mr. Spock told Captain Kirk ...

"Humans are highly illogical."

So, if the weighting of evidence and reasoning is not 50/50, then what is it?

We did a tremendous amount of research and looked into things never considered when we originally drafted the hypothesis for the Perfect Plan, but in the end, we discovered the true weighting.

We now know that the average person, when making a decision, does in fact process their conclusion based on evidence and reasoning, but in their minds, it translates into something slightly different. This little tweak helps us understand the weighting of each variable in the decision-maker's mind and the seemingly illogical stance that appeared to us at first.

We, as humans, don't necessarily process "Evidence + Reasoning." We actually simplify the formula, which translates for the *decision-making* process.

Instead of "Evidence + Reasoning = A Conclusion," it is actually:

Facts + Emotions = A Decision

Human beings review the facts and combine them with their emotions in order to generate their final decisions.

So, if this is true, what is the weighting between the two? Is it 50/50 like the legal system professes?

The answer might surprise you.

The percentage of a decision that is based on emotion is actually 85%. *But!* We *justify* the emotional part of the decision with just 15% of the known facts.

Wow! Think about it. Every decision we make is the result of facts and emotions, but we weight it with 85% emotion and only 15% facts.

The intriguing part is not the obvious emotional weighting, but the small amount of *justification*, which is combined with the facts. We use the facts to justify emotion, not the other way around.

So, if we are emotionally drawn to something and want to engage, that's fine, but we need to *justify* our emotional response before *acting* on the decision. Therefore, we need to focus on the justification part of the process. What does it mean to the decision-maker?

The study of the world's elite leaders' success in encouraging and predicting human behavior took us down paths we never dreamed of exploring. One such trail took us through the neurological sector of emotions. While emotions by their very nature appear to be far from logical, we learned that this was not in actuality true in application. As we dug deeper within the justification part of the process, another piece of the equation existed that brought sense to the Three Promises of the Perfect Plan.

As we justify an action that is stimulated by emotion, we found that there was a distinct correlation between the act of justification and the amount of the facts actually retained by the decision-maker. As we chased the path to understanding and ultimately the path to good news, we found another scientific truth:

The average person remembers only 6% of a presentation just 10 minutes after it is done!

To look at it from another angle, when you make a request or presentation to a person or a committee, they can recall only 6% of your work 10 minutes after you finished.

Wow. Bizarre but true.

A fun little test to prove the point is to watch a movie with someone from start to finish with no distractions. Enjoy and relax as if it was a routine night out. When the movie is done, wait for at least 10 minutes before asking a few questions. Make it go something like this:

"I really did enjoy the movie with you. It was one for the ages, and I am sure they have a shot at the Academy Award this year. I loved the plot and the writing was spectacular ... oh, by the way, what was the name of the main character? How about the other characters? Do you remember the name of the city where it took place?"

The results may shock you. Unless they consciously set out to memorize the facts and assuming it wasn't an epic like Harry Potter or a Spiderman movie set in NYC, they will recall only 6% of the details. You may be very capable of describing the plot, action and even the moral of the story, but in the end, the *facts* will leave you. This is where the other part of understanding falls into place.

We also learned that even though you can recall only 6% of the facts, you would always remember 100% of how you felt during the experience. This emotional retention, in essence, became the next piece of the puzzle.

Here is what we know.

People make decisions based on the sum of facts and emotions. Those emotions make up 85% of the decision, and they are justified with 15% of the facts. Yet, within 10 minutes after the decision or presentation, a person can recall only 6% of the facts, but they recall 100% of how they felt when they experienced the facts.

So, what are they teaching us?

It is all about how you *feel* when you use the product or make the decision. More importantly, it has to be *real* to them. Just because the average person recalls only 6% of what you say, that does not mean that the facts can be faked. It is just the opposite. What the best teams know is the truth behind the number. It has to do with the presenter, not the buyer.

The decision-maker or buyer needs to know the truth, but more so, they need to know that you, as the expert, are authentic. You see, the fact that the perspective buyer, or those you lead, retains only 6% of the presented facts is not a weakness but a strength, as long as the recipient understands that you — the presenter/leader — are a truthful expert. In turn, they do not have to know what you know … they simply trust your expertise so they can move on with their lives and past the decision.

In other words:

They want to outsource the success of their decision to you.

They do this because you have knowledge that they don't, nor are they willing to acquire it.

They need you but want to feel good about you as well.

As it turns out, the decision-maker is merely testing the presenter/leader to determine that they (the presenter/leader) know the product or issue better than anyone else. If they believe that you do, and they can feel good about their decision, you win!

This only happens if they know enough to feel good about your knowledge … get it?

It is a test.

Facts + Good Feelings about You = Justification
Justification = A Decision

It is all about *trusting you* with their personal success.

People, especially buying committees for large companies or teams of employees are actually looking to feel good about their decision (85%), but they need to justify it with the facts (15%).

In the end, they need to retain only 6% of those facts, because they feel good about *you as the leader.* It is *you* that they are trusting and *you* who they want to engage to make the project, product or service a success.

What they are telling you is that they want to have a 100% positive emotional recall about you as a person. That's enough to move ahead. They literally trust you to create success for the decision they just made. Be careful: You have to sincerely deliver and believe in your business and your product, or it will show through and they will never believe or trust you again.

In the end, they want to trust you but need to know that you trust yourself. That's a feeling that will carry both of you into the next stage of the relationship. The truth is the buyer does not want to know about your product as much as they want to feel 100% confident that you know your product and you can deliver.

You are the expert, and it is with you they trust their success.

Chapter 4 – Getting a Good Decision Lesson #1

Answer the Person, Not the Question

How do you give someone good advice or good understanding?

You answer the person, not the question.

In other words, the question often reveals more about the person asking the question than any response you may give.

This is a core concept that was shared and executed by everyone that fell into the Top 1% category. It does take a bit to digest because it turns *a reaction* into *an action.* To do so, you need to know another core belief:

When someone shows you who they really are, believe them!

When a person asks a question, in most cases, they are showing you who they really are and the Elite 1% know to believe them, and how to answer the question appropriately for the person who has been revealed.

This concept is not a means to sidestep or replace the truth; it is just the opposite.

This level of understanding creates the ability to answer the question with the truth that matters most to the person asking the question. The question may not, in itself, represent the real *reason it is being asked.* You have to be able to see past the question and look at the person asking it.

This step is a strategic application of the truth once you know that the asker really wants clear knowledge so they feel they have been given good advice, good understanding, or good news. To do this, the one answering the question has to be able to see past the question itself to what the question *says* about the asker.

How does he ask the question?

Why would she ask the question?

What reason exists to cause him to raise that point?

Knowing what drove the question will give you the insights into what *good* thing the asker is seeking.

For example, when the best of the best enter a boardroom or an environment where they are presenting themselves for any type of approval or award, they immediately know how a person will respond to their answers, regardless of the question. This is done because they understand as much if not more about the person asking the question than the question itself.

The first step in doing so is to know *who* the person asking the question really is and why they would ask the question. In other words, what is it about the people in the room that drives the question? The answer lies in knowing *who* it is that asked the question, and sometimes it is as simple as knowing what they do in the company and how they present themselves before they ask the question.

There are three classic groups of people in the world, and whoever recognizes these can answer the questions that are asked in a way that allows the decision-maker the best opportunity to process the truth. When you know *why* they asked the question to begin with, you can give them the answer that will most make sense to them.

Let's take a look at these groups.

Group #1 – The Foundation: the General Public, i.e. the Masses

The masses, the core of the general public, are the wonderful workers who make up the largest segment of the population today. They are good people who work hard but live paycheck to paycheck. They love their families, celebrate the holidays, and watch Monday Night Football. They exist through their heart, love good music, and happen to make up 80% of the world's population. They are the spirit that drives humanity forward and makes us great. It is to these people the world owes a tremendous gratitude. They supply the world with time, talent, and treasure, but there is something else interesting about them …

They are a very predictable group.

Politicians know it, the media knows it, and marketers know it. This is real.

So, how does this group, the masses, make decisions? If you knew the answer, you could build a model to support their needs. Economics 101 teaches us that where there is demand, we must create the supply. With this particular group of folks, if you to listen to how they ask the question, and you know *who* they are, it will always come back to the same answer.

So, what is the biggest driver in the decision- making process for the Foundation Class?

Price, i.e. cost.

It is the only answer they look toward, and the best of the best know it. Just ask the late Sam Walton, the founder of Wal-Mart. He knew it too. In fact, Wal-Mart tells you in their corporate logo's tag line every day – "Always low prices. Always."

The bottom line for this group of consumers is that almost every question about every decision comes down to price. Of course, *quality* of the product does weigh some in their minds as does *where* it was made, but in the end, it is all about *price*. The Elite 1% knows this, and they know it is as unarguable as certain laws of physics such as gravity and inertia. To the average buyer, those in the Foundation, it is simply all about price: Can I afford this?

You may argue with it, but your profound arguments still won't change the way it is.

The golden rule of leadership: Impress others, not yourself.

So, give them the price they need to build on the relationship, earn their trust and, above all, show your respect.

Group #2 – The Middles: Middle Class or Middle Managers

Some of the world's largest institutional business models are built on the predictability of this group, and to this day, it is shocking how few realize the impact they have on the global economy.

As we work through the social groups of decision- makers and purchasers, we quickly move beyond the Foundation (price seekers) and we come to the middle class. These are the folks who tend to be a little more educated — though not necessarily smarter — who lean toward a white-collar career and, after all is said and done, must *manage* other people in order to get things done. They are the social Middle Class and/or the corporate Middle Managers.

What we learned about this group was simple, yet profound. If you are in the "game" of leadership and marketing, understanding of this group is essential. The Middle Managers are competitive and always make their decisions based on:

Perception

Perception is the most important variable in a Middle's life, career, and social status. It is the driver and the basis of their decision-making process. Perception is a simple concept, and if you remember Lesson #1, you know how to answer their questions, because you know where they are coming from and what they desire.

The Middles, as we came to call them, are never concerned with price.

In their world, they are concerned only about how *others* perceive them and their decisions. In other words, it is not about how they think about themselves but about what others think about them.

So there lies the key we should question: Who are the *others*?

Are the others their own bosses or the ones they manage, i.e. the Foundation class we discussed in the section before?

Do they make righteous decisions that are good for the company?

Do they choose to do what is right for those around them, even if it means risk to themselves?

Are they worried about moving up or down the corporate food chain?

Are they most concerned about the way their employees see them?

Or, does it all boil down to keeping up with the Joneses?

The answer may not surprise you at all.

In truth, the answer is yes to both the corporate and social food chain and what others think about them.

They almost never think about putting others first. The concept of valor and selfless ambition to help others often eludes them.

In the end, their decisions are based solely on how the outcome will make them look, both up and down the corporate food chain. Sadly, this applies to corporate decisions, as well as personal decisions.

So, who are they trying to impress?

The Middles are driven by perception, and it goes both ways. They have a keen sense of awareness of the ebb and flow of management and society as it goes both up and down … or shall we say *through* them.

In their world, they are fixated on making sure those below them in the corporate or social hierarchy perceive their decisions as managerial, thus maintaining their integrity and credibility with those they manage. They are also concerned with making sure that those above them (corporately the Cs – CEO, CFO, CIO, etc.) believe and perceive them as worthy for promotion so that one day they can become a C as well, thus ultimately taking care of social progression as well.

The Middle Managers in the world are incredibly predictable because all they care about, regardless of the question or intent, is *perception*. They make strategic decisions based on their understanding of what is necessary to maintain their personal stature to the working class while also trying to make the upper echelon believe that they deserve to be one of them.

Those in the Elite 1% understand this principle and accept it to be true. They are then able to communicate and, in some ways, *sympathize* with the Middle Managers. This became a fundamental truth when we realized that the elite are able to see through their smokescreen and understand what questions the Middles are really asking. It is simple:

"How does this decision or action make me look?"

The lesson also relies on the understanding that Middle Managers don't always realize why they make the decisions they do. Thus, the presenter/leader who is enlightened by the Perfect Plan can wade through the irrelevant issues and get down to what is most important to the client. The best of the best know that perception is combated only with other laws of behavior, eerily similar to the laws of physics: Matter cannot be created or destroyed, just reshaped or reformed.

Translated into more mundane terms of leadership and marketing, perception is always the motivation for a decision and is always present. Best of all, it is easy to recognize, because it often takes the form of a *brand.*

Brands mean more than anything.

Brands are perceptions.

Brands translate into low-risk decisions that no one complains about. Some of the greatest marketing brands of all time have been conceived and deployed based on this law of behavior.

Just ask Fidelity Investments.

Fidelity runs one of the highest quality families of mutual funds, and without question, some of the best and brightest people in the world work there. For more than four decades, Fidelity has taken care of Americans' retirement plans, investments, and trusts. Best of all, they are really, really good. They are also really, really smart and totally understand the Middles. This is what allows them to market based on the power of the Fidelity brand.

The proof is in the pudding. For years, IBM has been the dominant technology hardware player when it comes to sales and distribution. They are brilliant and deserve every client they acquire, because not only do they do a wonderful job, they also understand what others don't — the decision to award large corporate contracts is not made by the Cs (CEO, CFO, CIO, etc.), but a committee of Middle Managers. So, since the Middles make decisions based only on perception — both up and down — and the word "perception" is best translated to "brand." IBM built an empire by capitalizing on their *brand*.

IBM is brilliant.

On the first day of IBM sales school, all new reps are taught the greatest sales line in history: *"No one has ever been fired for buying an IBM."*

Once they had established themselves as a global brand, they had it won. They knew that when a committee of Middle Managers met to decide on contracts and to whom they would award the biggest opportunities, IBM was a sure winner. They had quality products, low risk, and a recognizable brand. They made the ultimate marketing hat trick.

Fortunately, IBM never wavered from a commitment of excellence, and they were able to take their brand and superior work into a market that was looking for something stable and trustworthy — something that would not destroy careers or credibility. IBM now does trillions of dollars of business with the world's best companies because they understood Middle Managers make decisions on *perception* and perception really means *brands*. IBM also understood the lesson mentioned earlier: That people, by making a decision, trust you with that decision's success. IBM delivered.

No one, up or down, ever questions a solid brand, and therefore the *perception* the Middle Manager craves is accomplished. The Middle Managers appear smart to the Foundation working class and reliable to the upper class. Perception is created and saved, and a decision is executed.

Group #3 – The Cs (CEO, CFO, CIO, etc.) and the Upper Class

What does your landscaper have in common with a Wall Street CEO?

Let's find out.

As we studied and worked our way up the corporate and social ladder of decision makers, the field became narrower as we reached the apex: The Cs and Upper Class reign supreme.

The upper class, both social and corporate, is made up of a unique and dynamic group of ladies and gentlemen. They are usually hard workers who sacrifice a lot in their lives to make it to the top. They are bright, well-educated, sometimes smarter, and usually deserve the position they have obtained.

The Cs, by their very nature, make their decisions differently than the other two groups, i.e. the Foundations and the Middles. The Top 1% of the world's leaders, sales and marketing teams understand this concept because, in many ways, they evolved through the same social and corporate system and along a similar path. However, there is a difference in attainability that we will discuss later.

It quickly came to our attention that the Cs, while they may seem mysterious and untouchable, are actually the easiest to understand. The decision- making process is the same for this group no matter how they made it through the mud and muck of social and corporate climbing. It does not matter if they were born to it, or simply developed the maturity to attain it. Either way, the Cs based their decision on one thing alone: Return on Investment.

(ROI)

It sounded cold until we unlocked their secret, already known to the Elite 1%. It also seemed a bit to mechanical and quantitative, but there was more to their story.

What we came to discover is that the pinnacle of social and corporate structures actually makes   decisions in a similar manner as the base group (the Foundation) but with a slight twist. Instead of *price,* the core concept to reach the Cs is the return they receive on their *investment.*

The Elite 1% of leadership, sales, and marketing professionals implemented everything they knew about life when dealing with the Cs. The basic principle and key concept of answering the *person* and not the *question* still reigned true. They wanted to give and get good advice, understanding, and news. For the best of the best, the *who* in this case is always simple to determine, so before answering their questions, the Elite 1% asked one of their own to the Cs:

"What exactly is your investment?"

We were shocked at first, then it all made sense.

In 100% of the test and trials, the Cs answered the question in the way the top 1% knew they would. Investment is *not* a monetary term or an accounting issue to the Cs. To them, the word "investment" means "time."

Literally, clock time … tick, tock, tick, tock.

The C's wanted to know what the return was on the *time* spent and allocated to the deal. In other words, "Is this the best use of our talents, assets, and dollars in coordination with the allotment of time it takes to successfully complete the project?"

Once this is established, they can then ask, "What do we get in return?"

Wow!

Ironically, we had heard this concept before, and you would never guess where.

In most suburbs, it seemed that on some days, every other truck you see is a landscape vehicle. These are the hard-working men and women who make the world look better by transforming our yards and corporate centers into freshly groomed portraits of beauty. They have redefined our expectations surrounding the way things should look, and the images we should portray. Simply put, they make it a beautiful place to live. The landscapers are the people who keep life green and clean when no one seems to notice. Ironically, few people give them the credit they deserve … everyone that is, except the Cs.

Thirty years ago, the world was a different place. If anyone told you that TVs would be flat, we would pay for water in bottles, or that 5th graders would have cell phones, you would have laughed them off the street. Better yet, if you were told that almost every home in

America would pay for someone other than the 13-year-old boy down the street to cut their grass, you would be equally humored. Yet it happened.

What caused such an evolution that it has come to define our interpretation of success?

Did anyone, other than the Top 1%, ever ask why?

Well, the truth was there, and it was the same truth today that the Cs understand about their decision- making process, and most importantly about the idea of *time.*

As the market and demand for landscapers grew to such large proportions, it became obvious to the insiders that it was never about cutting grass, but all about "buying back" valuable time. While it is true that most people enjoy yard work and might actually enjoy cutting their own grass, the time allocation required versus the cost that the landscapers charge is the best return on your investment. If you don't believe me, ask yourself a question. If you cut your own yard, how much time per week do you spend to make it look its best? Two hours? Three or four hours?

OK, reverse the question. How long would it take a landscaper to do an equal or better job for you? 45 minutes? An hour?

Next, unless you are retired or find landscaping your primary form of exercise or therapy, how much does the four or five hours you spend taking care of your own yard mean to you? Can you use that four or five hours for something else? Can that time be better spent with your family or working on something more productive and even income- related?

If the answer is yes, how much would you spend to buy those four or five hours? What could you make once you have the time back?

You see, time really is money and a deployment of precious resources. So, you need to know *how* the time is being spent and the opportunity cost associated with it.

The Cs — corporate officers, business owners, and those who have reached a certain level of social and structural maturity — make decisions based on the allocation of the resources necessary to make the best and most desired return. The most valuable of these resources has not changed in a thousand years. It is *time* itself.

The Top 1% has grown accustomed to this and understands the process better than anyone. They know not to approach the Cs with a low-cost offer because *price is for the masses*. They also know that *brand carries little weight with the Cs* because they aren't interested in what others think about them. They just want *to understand performance as it relates to the allocation of time* and resources.

In some ways, the decision-making process of the Cs is the easiest to understand. It is about quality and the impact the proposed project has on their mission, not what others think or how cheap it is. The Top 1% knows this and respects the Cs by giving them a different approach to the offer. The Top 1% serves the Cs best, by helping them grow and accomplish their mission, regardless of price or brand. It is about the best quality for the maximum performance of the time spent on the project.

In the end, one of the most profound things we learned from the elite teams was how to understand the reasoning behind why people make the decisions they do. The first step in the process is to know *who* that person was and where they fit in the corporate or social hierarchy.

If you know *who*, then you know *why*.

That is the foundation of enlightenment that takes you on the path toward the Perfect Plan but before we get to that, there are a few more lessons to learn.

Chapter 5 – Getting a Good Decision Lesson #2

Who Is In Charge?

The second lesson we learned leading up to the Perfect Plan seemed to fly in the face of traditional leadership, sales and marketing training, but by now, we were expecting these lessons to defy accepted practices.

The Top 1% know that by asking another simple question, "Who is in charge of the meeting?", things begin to change.

By "meeting," we mean any meeting — sales, leadership, marketing, social and professional. Whenever two or more people gather together for a purpose, a congress forms. Then, as dynamics develop, planned or unplanned, the opportunity exists for leadership to rise up.

So, let's ask:

Who is in charge of the meeting … any meeting?

The answer is simple:

The person in charge of a meeting, any meeting, is the person who is being judged by the outcome of the decision.

Please repeat this in your mind and even re-read it a few times — it is one of the most critical factors leading up to the Perfect Plan:

The person in charge is the person being *judged* by the outcome of the decision.

So, how do you know who that person is? The process is rather simple as long as you don't underestimate anyone in the room. For the best example, let's go back and finish a story that's become famous in the Perfect Plan universe.

$450,000,000.00 is a lot of money.

It is a story I have used to painstakingly illustrate the power of the Perfect Plan and the unfair advantage it gave us.

As it is today, at the time of the story, we dominated our field and with such a significant win, we felt we were on top of the world.

As you may recall from Chapter 1 of this book, after we had finished our presentation and executed perfectly all three lessons of a good decision and the full force of the Perfect Plan, the CEO came around the boardroom table to congratulate us on our win that day. She noted our professionalism and told us that she felt sorry for the other two teams who were still scheduled to present after us. She even went so far as to ask that we return the following Monday to begin transitional work and even offered a celebration dinner for us the following night. It was simply the best feeling in the world … a $450 million win!

Later that night, I met the broker who had referred the business to us for our customary celebration cocktail that I like to call "Daddy's Lil' Helper." (Gentleman Jack on the rocks, splash of cola and a lime.) As I looked up from the bar, I saw my friend and longtime colleague walking toward me. Yet, instead of the celebration I was expecting, I could see instantly by the look on his face that something was wrong.

He had news, and it was not good.

He sat down, and I knew he had been given one of the hardest jobs in the world. He had to tell me that they (the committee) had reversed their original decision to award the business to us. Basically, he had to take away our win and award it to someone else.

He was kind and sincere as he broke the news to me. Best of all, he was willing to tell me about a mistake we never realized had been made.

My mind immediately grew foggy as he spoke, and before I knew the real reason of our loss, I began to forecast illusions and create irrational excuses in my head. In a split second that seemed like an eternity, I wanted to commit the worse crime any leader could do and seek to blame something (or someone) other than myself. Fortunately, the thoughts were fleeting and before he could finish his initial apology, I had snapped back to my senses.

I knew I was responsible no matter what happened, and I would take the blame. I became excited knowing anything he could tell me from here forward was a gift. I needed to know how to prevent such a loss from happening again, so I needed to know what we had done correctly, and what we needed to do better next time. Plain and simple, all I could do now was be humble and prepare for the next time. I knew my job as a leader was not to seek perfection, but growth – simply put, I needed to learn how we could be "always becoming."

There is a saying we have at the Perfect Plan:

"99% of academics can be beaten by 1% of politics any day."

We knew this concept well, so we strived hard to cover both sides of this pendulum, knowing that while we can't control the politics, we can trust the academics. We consider the Perfect Plan to fall on the academic side of the pendulum. We had worked too hard on this deal and rehearsed it too many times for it to come down to a sloppy mistake. I was hoping the reason for such an unprecedented reversal was politics, but unfortunately it was not.

My buddy got straight to the point, and I appreciated his candor. He was as shocked as I me, and even though the CEO had already awarded us the victory, she reversed it shortly after we left and went another direction.

"Why?" I asked.

"You would not have believed it," he told me. Immediately after the presentation and the award, we walked out of the boardroom together and proceeded less than 45 feet to the elevator. He congratulated us on our victory, but by the time he returned, the room had changed.

"I was amazed at how quickly they turned the mood around," my friend told me. "By the time I was back in the room, they had reversed their decision and wanted to see the other options."

"Why?" I asked.

"Well, it was the IT guy," he informed me. "It was he who actually sank the deal by saying the most dreaded any committee could hear, and they responded."

By the way, this committee, with the exception of the CEO, was made up exclusively of Middles. Everyone on the committee was represented as middle managers, and we were prepared. We had worked tirelessly to frame the presentation for their decision-making process, i.e. brand awareness.

I was astonished. "What could he have possibly said to reverse a CEO's decision and influence an entire group of middle managers so quickly?"

My friend soberly quoted the IT Manager, who said, "'If we move forward with this, we will be judged poorly by the outcome of our decision.'"

There it was. He threw an atomic bomb of *perception* into the minds of the Middles, and it worked. They ran like the wind.

He killed the deal. He reversed all the momentum, and it cost us dearly.

The IT Guy, after not saying a single word during the entire presentation, became the most powerful person in the room and the person in charge. All because his perception of the outcome would create a poor judgment on him, personally and professionally.

For a quick review, we know that middle managers make decisions on the perception they think others have about them. We also learned that the most powerful person in the room is the one being judged by the outcome of the decision.

So, it all came down to a single moment in time. The middle-manager IT executive, who was concerned about how others would perceive him, preyed upon those truths influencing the other Middles in the room, sending a resounding message that was received quite readily. They, the committee, turned and ran from the idea of "we will be judged poorly by the outcome of this decision."

A double whammy!

While I knew the decision was made and committees rarely reversed a direction once set upon, I had to ask what it was that made the IT Manager think the way he did, and why he felt compelled to share it with the committee.

"It was simple," my friend explained. "While not part of the presentation, the website was not to his liking, and he felt his employees and peers would judge him poorly if they went in that direction."

"You have to be kidding me!" I blurted out. "For $450 million, I will build him whatever website he wants!"

"I know," my friend told me. "But the seed was planted, and they moved on."

So this is where it really hurts. I asked him who they decided to go with and how did they address the web issue I had overlooked. I never thought it to be a factor in the decision-making process. (My mistake, for sure).

"Well, the team they chose never showed a website. They just mentioned in passing that they could build whatever he wanted."

So, there it was … while we had failed, we actually validated one of the key lessons we had learned in the trials of the Perfect Plan.

The Middles care only about how they are perceived to others, and the person in charge was the person who was being judged by the outcome of the decision.

In this case, the way the IT Manager delivered his fear to the committee was so broad-based that the rest filled in their own mental blanks of perception and reversed the decision. The CEO was in a terrible position. If she overruled the committee, she was sending them a message that they were wrong and would squash future creativity from the group. Thankfully, she herself was one of the Top 1%; she knew better than to try.

The Lessons are like laws of physics. You might not fully agree with the result, but don't argue with them … you will lose.

What did we learn?

Well, with a 95% success rate from the Perfect Plan principles, we knew this was part of the 5%. However, in an odd way, we were excited. This loss only helped fortify in our minds that the Perfect Plan was the secret to the world's best, and we —regardless of how good we were at the time — are just as subject to the lessons and principles as anyone else. We overlooked someone and underestimated him. We failed to understand who the most important person was in the room that day. It cost us in the moment, but the future payout would be huge.

We were excited with what we had learned because we applied another simple truth we discovered along the way. After every meeting —win or lose — we ask two questions of our own team:

1. What did we do right today?
2. What could we do better next time?

The Top 1% had taught us that you never ask what you did *wrong* or all you will ever do is second-guess yourself.

If you are the best, you should believe that you did everything possible given the time, talent and effort you had to be your best. If you fall short, that's OK, but celebrate what you did right and learn what you can do better next time. We did, and our close rate soon grew to 98%!

Chapter 6 – Getting a Good Decision Lesson #3

Bringing It All Together Before the Plan

As we have learned so far, the Perfect Plan is based on a few fundamental absolutes that help prepare you for the Plan itself. We know that all anyone really wants in life is an unfair advantage. We learned that Good Advice leads to Good Understanding, and then to Good News.

Facts + Emotion = A Decision

We discovered that people make their decisions based on 85% emotion, but justify it with 15% of the facts.

We know that after a presentation, the average person recalls only 6% of what you said but 100% of how they felt about you when you presented it.

Good Feelings about You + Facts = Justification
Justification = A Decision

We now know that if you know *who* someone is, you then know *why* they make the buying decisions they do.

We learned the most important lesson of all: The person in charge is the person being judged by the outcome of the decision.

OK then, let's bring it all together.

The Top 1% of the world's leadership, sales and marketing teams follow a distinctive plan that sets the decision-maker into a position of making the favorable choice for their team. The Perfect Plan is the sequence of events that forms a presentation style that allows these teams to stand out above all others, but it's founded on the fundamental truths listed above. These truths are scientifically proven and, until fundamentally shaken from their perch, need to be treated as if they were physical laws of nature. You might not agree or understand them, but they are nevertheless true. If you respect them, as the Top 1% does, you can build on a formula that guarantees success.

Before every presentation and meeting, the best individuals and teams spend hours building their case before they ever dream of deploying the Perfect Plan. To do so, each of the fundamentals listed above are vetted and displayed in order to avoid any mistakes or miscues. "War rooms" are built and designed so that these functions can be graphed, charted, and displayed. Multiple views are taken and talent levels grow and advance everyone, but the simplest thing of all is the most important to know.

Asking "who?" and "why?"

Remember, decisions are based on 85% emotion and justified with 15% of the facts from which you remember only 6%, but you recall 100% of how you felt.

In the past, these numbers did not exist, so all of the weighting was placed on emotion and how you felt, but it was misguided by the belief that you should expose the negatives of a client's current situation and show them their "pain" in order to motivate them to change. Looking back, it is amazing anything was ever accomplished in leadership, sales and marketing, but as cultures adapt, people became immune to any particular phenomena, so it either grows or dies. In this case, the archaic "pain" technique of leadership and marketing seems to be fading to a slow death, and that's a wonderful thing.

For a very, very long time, the Top 1% have avoided these "disturb" or "pain" techniques because they always knew that the client is looking to them to *know* their business. That's why clients remember only 6% of what is said, because they don't *need* to remember everything as long as they believe the presenter knows what she is doing. If they, the prospect, knew as much as you do about the product, they don't need you. As stated before, they are trusting you with their success. They need you, but you have to earn it. It has to be real, genuine, and sincere. No faking it.

The Top 1% also knows that even though their clients recall only 6% of the data, they remember 100% of how they felt about the presentation. So think about it. If the lessons leading up to the Perfect Plan are true, and the prospects recall 100% of how they felt when they were with you, why in the world would anyone want to create an environment based on fear and pain? In other words, the "disturb and motivate" guys did a great job of making the client uncomfortable with their situation — which was, ironically, their goal. Yet when the client did decide to make a change, they routinely decided to do it with someone other than the presenter! They went a different direction, choosing to award the business to someone else. Why? Because all they remember about the presenters is how they felt, which was bad!

On the way to successfully creating pain by disturbing their prospect, they also created an association of that pain with themselves. It became Pavlovian.

Ivan Pavlov was a Russian psychiatrist who founded the reflex conditioning theory. He believed that people responded by reflex (i.e., learned habits) to certain conditions.

His study became famous for experiments that involved ringing a dinner bell before feeding his dogs. After some time, the dogs would slobber from just hearing the bell ring as the sound brought instant anticipation of food.

Ivan went on to prove (evidence and reasoning) that certain conditions can stimulate a response purely on a learned reflex. Well, guess what? He was right, but Western leadership over the past 40 years has misinterpreted its use in the art of influencing human behavior. The only thing that came of it was the classical sales training of the 1960s through the late 1980s (some still linger today) that utilized these negative techniques to motivate behavior.

These actions may have motivated a change in behavior, but the individual in question often reflexively went with someone other than the original presenter. In their efforts to change, they migrated to someone less painful because they associated the disturbance with that original presenter.

I had a unique inside track of an effort to prove that the disturb-and-motivate techniques do not work. For years, I have had the pleasure of serving at the Summit Counseling Center in Atlanta, Georgia as Chairman and Board President. Summit is a fantastic organization that delivers over 7,000 clinical hours per year in counseling to help people through rough times and out of dark places.

With the leverage that my position provided, we decided to incorporate the academic strength of some of their best and brightest counselors and doctors. We went to them with a simple question: Is there a list of emotions, broken down between "good" and "bad"?

Basically, we wanted to target the good emotions and discover their opposite "bad" emotions. Once completed, we would be able to visualize them, track and study their use in a scientific manner that revealed their counter balance.

As we began to list these conditions, we found that there were more emotions than anyone could reasonably track. That's when I realized that the list was right under our noses. I had just finished a fantastic book by Allen Hunt. Allen is an old friend and a wonderful guy who happens to have a Ph.D. from Yale in First Century and New Testament studies. His book, *The Fruit-Full Living*, focused on a first century bad guy who turned good — Saul, better known as the Apostle Paul.

In one of Paul's many letters from the time, most of which make up the New Testament, he actually did our work for us. We discovered that he had laid out list in perfect sequence.

When Paul was communicating back and forth to his many churches, he wrote one letter that listed the emotions and character he felt everyone should try to achieve. He did this knowing that even the most negative and harmful individuals could not argue with these essential feelings. Once we realized how perfectly suited this list was to the study, we knew we were on to something. Paul spelled out what we know refer to as "The Fruit of the Spirit," as such:

1. Love
2. Joy
3. Peace
4. Patience
5. Kindness
6. Goodness
7. Gentleness
8. Self-control

Some 2,000 years before the first behavioral economist came into existence, Paul actually created a structure that allows one emotion to build upon the next in such a way that virtually 100% of psychiatrists today agree with the progression. For example, once you have love, you then find peace. Once you have peace, you find patience, and with patience, you find kindness, and so on. They build upon each other, and neither can exist without the other before it. We found the list perfect for our study.

We then asked the best doctors and counselors specializing in human behavior and mental wellness to discuss the probability of the list's genius. All agreed on its findings, and no one questioned the power of the sequence. Yet, even when we discovered the validity and power of the positive thoughts, we were still concerned about those who focus on the "negative" emotions to influence others. So, we asked the same group of doctors to review the "good" list and to attach the opposite emotion to each corresponding good emotion. Frankly, the results shocked us.

For example, I thought the opposite of love was hate, but it's actually *fear*. I thought the opposite of joy was sadness, but it is really loneliness. The toughest was the opposite of self-control, which is hopelessness. If you don't believe me, just ask any addict.

The complete list is given below:

Good Emotions	Bad Emotions
Love	Fear
Joy	Loneliness
Peace	Anxiety
Patience	Uncertainty
Kindness	Lack of Respect
Goodness	Envy
Gentleness	Lost
Self-Control	Hopelessness

From here, with a new basis for communication and understanding, we began to watch and observe. It became quickly and overwhelmingly apparent what was happening. Once we had our barometer (the list above), we could see clearly when certain leadership and marketing individuals (who were not in the Top 1%) jumped over to the right side of the chart and began the disturb and motivate process. It became so obvious that you could see them strategically build up momentum toward the negative as these folks purposely created an environment driven and fueled by bad emotions.

The tracked results were predictable and a bit surprising as well. The close ratios of the sales teams who created bad feelings were higher than had we expected, at approximately 8%. As you can guess, however, our follow-up discussions and surveys with the clients followed a foreseeable theme. Several of the clients were motivated to make a change when presented with negative theme, but close to 100% of those did not engage the teams that used the disturb-and-motivate techniques. They cited a "bad feeling" when recalling the presentation of the team and translated it to the individual. Many went on to say that they had enough crises in their day-to-day business activities and they had no desire to invite someone into their world that seemed to make them feel distracted and demotivated. More than one case study went on to explain that the disturb- and-motivate team eventually made him feel stupid for making what he felt historically was a right decision.

As you can guess, those cases we studied involving the Elite 1%, who never deployed a disturb-and-motivate strategy, were the exact opposite in their results. We watched in amazement as the best stayed on the "good" side of the emotional fence the entire time they were presenting. Even when the realities of a challenge would surface, they brought it back to the "good" side, regardless of how bad the challenge may have been. The science was once again backed up as we determined the successful close ratio of the Elite 1% who used the "good" to motivate change was 95%. Indeed, the exit interviews with the prospects were overwhelmingly focused on the positive feelings they had about the Elite 1% team and their message. They felt confident that the better teams were real experts, and they could deliver. They seemed magnetized to the team's good nature and positive aspect. They even, on several occasions, gave us unsolicited compliments, eerily listing the positive emotions as if they had seen our chart.

This is the point where it all begins and where Plans are executed … Perfect Plans.

Chapter 7 – The Promises of the Perfect Plan

As we discussed in the brief of Chapter 2, the Perfect Plan is the organized, proven process followed by the world's Elite 1% of leadership, sales and marketing professionals. It is the combination of their sincere work that is based on lessons previously discussed that neutralize any distractions, allowing complete focus on the presentation.

This is where the magic happens.

This is the "secret sauce."

Simply put, the Perfect Plan is a proven process involving a series of Three Promises and Three Beliefs that collide during a presentation so the prospective buyer or decision-maker can affirmatively answer three simple questions in their mind. Then and only then can the engagement begin and the purest relationships emerge.

Let's examine each of the Three Promises and see how they eventually collide with the Three Beliefs to create the Perfect Plan.

Promise #1 – Gratification, an Attitude of Gratitude

When you become aware of the proven process and the patterns of the Perfect Plan, the first of these Promises quickly becomes apparent. Any competitor will agree that the most critical action of any game or contest is always the first move. Traditionally, it is where one of the parties involved tries to command the high ground and thus gain a classical advantage. Ironically, this is not so with the Elite 1%. Their first move is seemingly in the opposite direction. Their first move is to create a feeling of humble and sincere *gratification*, with heartfelt thankfulness demonstrated to the client or those they are to lead.

The first step is designed to genuinely reverse the field and give the prospect the high ground by letting them know that you are grateful and thankful for their time, effort, work, and their very existence. In its purest form, it is the beginning of a relationship founded upon an Attitude of Gratitude. It is pure grace, and it is sincere. It cannot be faked, and it must be true. When it happens, something special begins to grow in the hearts of everyone involved.

Let's look at a few examples.

Anyone who has ever seen an Academy Awards presentation ceremony, better known as the Oscars, will know that the acceptance speeches all start with "I would like to thank." This is where the winner begins to list all the people who "helped them get to where they are tonight" and those "who made it all possible."

We have all heard these lines before, and for most of the audience, it is the point where we get to see *who* the actors really are and where their appreciation is founded. Most of the speeches are genuine and sincere with a humble gratitude and a few tears of joy. Occasionally, we do get to hear one that is so off-key that a little sleep sets in because some actors can't rescue themselves from a verbal flop. No one is there to help them by yelling, "Cut!" While it might mean something to those actors who are reading from their prepared lists, it really does nothing for the audience. That's where we came in and decided to ask:

Why does it work for some and not for others?

For some, the names they read are in thankful cadence but never seem to make it past the viewer's ear. It is just chatter to the millions who are at home watching and waiting for the night to unfold. But why is that? What is it about those movie stars' personas that turn your attention away? We watch their movies, so why can't we watch their speeches? It's simple.

There is a disconnect between you and the seemingly *insincere* words that have nothing whatsoever to do with you. While the Oscars seem to magnetize you to the show itself, there are a few award winners whose lack of personal connection drives your conscience away. Without the ability to bond with them, there is no appreciation for their words. They become talking heads who never make it into the consciousness of the viewers.

The best know better, and those special moments, even as distant as they, both physically and personally, become something special. They employ the Perfect Plan with a strong emphasis on Promise #1.

Genuine, sincere, and heartfelt *Gratification*, on the other hand, is something uniquely wonderful while remaining different altogether. Though not exclusively our own discovery, the best of the best found that the act of sincere gratification is the emotion that bonds two people together. When someone is truly appreciating to another, they become inseparable.

60

More than any other single emotion, activity, or stimulant, gratification is the strongest element in the human mind.

A study from the University of North Carolina at Chapel Hill confirmed what we already knew was true. Their researchers had a hypothesis, and a very simple question to test it. They wanted to know a secret, so they researched couples who had been married to each other for over 60 years. The research focus was centered on the key to their longevity in matrimony. Simply put, the researchers wanted to know what kept the couples together so long. Is there one thing that they did differently than anyone else? The answer was a resounding yes. They were different.

One hundred percent of the couples studied revealed that they had built their relationship on an Attitude of Gratitude. Each subject said, in almost unanimous fashion, that they felt their spouse had a deep and sincere appreciation for them. They were genuinely thankful for each other and, as a result, have been able to *bond* for over 60 years.

These couples obviously had ups and downs over the decades, but it was their mutual attitude of gratitude that got them through it together. It was the secret to their success.

So, of all the emotions possible, the one that bonds two people — or organizations — together, more than any other, is gratification. The Attitude of Gratitude creates a bond that builds and builds with no end in sight. It becomes a connection that glues people together indefinitely.

We were reinforced by a proof that the Top 1% already knew and had established. We went back to the same set of doctors who revealed the Paulininan chart of emotions to find that gratitude releases a chemical response in the brain, which caused enormous bonding to occur between the recipient and the person who cause the appreciation. In other words, a bonding occurs when there is an obvious and sincere thankfulness expressed for a person's presence and very being.

We were happily amazed as we studied the best, who already knew this lesson and had incorporated the concept into every presentation and every meeting they attended. Every action, conversation, and presentation starts with an Attitude of Gratitude, or what I like to refer to as a Face of Grace. It is a sequence that becomes so magnetic that the recipient is compelled to bond with you on unconscious levels.

The first action taken by the Elite 1% is not to attack or take the high ground. The first act is one of humble grace that sincerely bonds them to the prospect. They do it with an act of gratitude.

Promise #2 – Clear Education

Once you have established a bond through *gratification*, you begin *educating*.

Education, within the Perfect Plan, is a little different than what you may have been exposed to in the outside world. So many people approach me during a Relationship Training Course and ask, "What do we say? What do we talk about?"

I often respond, "I have no idea, but pick something and let's talk about it."

True as that is, there is a key to increased success that we learned from the Elite 1%. Their magic was founded on the premise that they never pick more than three things to talk about at any one time. You see, the Elite 1% know that humans typically only remember three things from any given conversation or presentation. Those who speak English are a perfect example.

Adults have a short attention span and this limits the number of things they can focus on at any one time. So, the study taught us to pick three things (and only three things!) that you need to educate your audience on and to lightly, ever so lightly, cover those topics. If you keep it to three, your success rate will climb to new heights. The goal here isn't to impress them with facts, figures, and reams of data. It is about building trust.

Here's the truth.

The people you are talking to, those you are trying to convince to take action, rarely care which three things you choose to discuss. They have not come there to relive a college exam, nor do they want a lecture. What they really want to know is: Are you trustworthy?

Can you be trusted?

If so, then they can take steps toward the real reason you are there — to trust you with what you *haven't* said.

Here's why.

Today's business-to-business environment lives in a state of constant crisis.

Most businesses are either in a crisis, leaving a crisis, or running toward a crisis.

They certainly don't need more crises in their lives.

So, what they really want is to trust you with their success once they believe you are the expert they can trust. Better yet, they never want to become the expert themselves.

All people really want is to know that you are the expert and they can recall enough to justify that you are who you say you are, even if you have not said that much.

This is provable.

As you now know, a decision is the product of Evidence + Reasoning, or better said, Facts + Emotion.

This is important to understand.

People may remember only 6% of the three things that you say, but they remember every emotion they *feel* while they are with you. In other words, they will recall 100% of how you made them feel after they forgot most of what you said.

How many times have you returned home from an activity where you can't recall everything you did but certainly recalled how you felt when you did it?

This holds true not only in activities and memory recall but in your use of language and numbers as well.

Interestingly enough, we found that every time you use a number in a presentation you risk losing half your audience. This applies to leadership meetings, discussions, and domestic and international sales as well.

People have an incredibly hard time following a train of numbers during a presentation, and when presented with a multitude of facts, they begin to mentally check out of the process. When this is combined and over-seeded with the actual topics you are educating them with, it can become a deadly combination.

During our study, we found that keeping any presentation to three topics or fewer was the perfect number for success. When pushed beyond three, the law of diminishing returns became evident.

Our study proved that whenever a person receives three topics to digest, it sets the baseline for success, but when a fourth topic is added, the probability drops by 25%. When a fifth is added, it drops by 50%, and a sixth topic creates a total crash with a diminishing return rate close to 0%. So, what does it tell you?

Go back to basics. *The prospect is not looking to be educated in the classical sense.* What they want is to be educated on the *good news.* It is the validation that you know the material so they don't have to.

They are literally listening in order to *justify* their decision.

As we discussed, decisions are the sum of evidence and reasoning or simply put, facts + emotion. The decision is based on 85% emotion but justified with 15% of the facts. Additionally, 10 minutes after your audience leaves the room, they will recall only about 6% of everything you said, but they remember 100% of how they felt when you said it. (Shall I repeat it again?)

So, there you go ... they don't want to know as much as you think they do, so maximize the probability of success and respect their roles in the process. Pick three things and stick to it.

The Elite 1% knows this very well. When they pick three things to talk about, they choose the ones that create an emotion founded on trust. The prospect or team member you are leading may leave the meeting trying to remember what you said, but they know with 100% certainty that they totally trust you and believe that you will deliver. You are the expert they need for the project's success and will follow your lead.

Of course, you need to explain what they need to know, but only the extent they are expecting to absorb it. Ultimately, it is about creating trust. "I don't need to know everything as long as you do; I'm good with that and I trust you." This is the attitude you are trying to build.

The education step in the Perfect Plan is the biggest challenge most people face. Too many times, leaders fall backward in their thinking. For more than 25 years, I have worked with brilliantly smart leaders, sales and marketing people, and it is common to see them stumble and make simple mistakes in this area. It is easy to do.

So many people are tempted and commit their cardinal sin in the area of *education*. They seem more interested in impressing themselves than their client. This is when we might witness a classic "show up and throw up" maneuver. It occurs when a leadership or sales person feels compelled to tell the prospect everything he or she knows, even if it takes all day and covers hundreds of irrelevant topics. It is usually the key ingredient to any failure. It is difficult, even for the well-trained professionals, to restrain themselves, and that is what makes this step so hard.

Your job is to win their trust by making the complex seem simple, without taking away from the integrity of the subject matter.

Ultimately, that is all the client really wants and longs to hear.

Steve Jobs said it best when he referred to how difficult it is to take difficult subject matter and simplify it for the consumer. In a Business Week interview in 1998, he said, *"That's been one of my mantras — focus and simplicity. Simple can be harder than complex: You have to work hard to get your thinking clean to make it simple. But it's worth it in the end because once you get there, you can move mountains."*

The Elite 1% begins each presentation with an Attitude of Gratitude that builds a bond. Then they build an environment that creates an education of understanding. In other words, it is the "I get it!" moment. Do you remember a time in your life when the light bulb flipped on and you said those words? Do you recall what it was you *got*? Perhaps you can't remember the details, but I bet you recall 100% of how you *felt* when you got it.

Education is about justification and the good news that comes with it.

Promise #3 – Ease of Business

The Third Promise and the final step in the presentation sequence is that the Elite 1% relieve the client of any burdens.

We simply call this *Ease of Business*.

In our research, we determined that the best leaders, managers, and marketing professionals followed these three Promises in the *exact order* to create the Perfect Plan. You must start with the Attitude of Gratitude and then move to a clear Education, before making it simple and *Easy* for them to get on board and advance the deal.

People are busy and already feel their lives are complicated. Most people and businesses live from one challenge to another. As we learned in the Education Promise, they are either headed toward a crisis, in the middle of a crisis, or just leaving a crisis. Either way, they don't need another crisis, and they will balk if that is what you offer them.

What they need is someone who is going to make their life a little bit easier. If your offer makes it easy, simple, and crisis-free, they will engage in it with lightning speed. This generates an emotion of liberation, like a vast burden has been lifted from their shoulders. You want them to think, that whenever they are with you, "It is so easy!"

Once again, the Elite 1% start with the bonding emotion of gratitude, continuing toward the facts of justifying and educating, then close with the emotion of relief.

Have you ever had someone step in and just solve a problem that you believed would never get resolved? Have you ever had a deadline that you didn't think you could meet when someone stepped in and made it easy? Remember the feelings? Immediately, either consciously or subconsciously, you felt like you could work with this person and, indeed, wanted to work with them. The relief someone feels by knowing their life is easier because of you is joyful.

Being the one who provides the relief makes you a hero!

Ken Hunnington, the CEO of Response Mine Interactive in Atlanta, often talks about the transition from the "sale to the application" as being the most critical step of any business. "People are sold something that never seems to do as it is advertised, so they become trained to prepare for the worse," Ken says. In today's business-to-business world, he says, "the translation of this feeling might build an emotional response associated with regret or anxiety for any future association. It is up to those who are in the elite field of leadership to create a safe environment where everyone trusts that they are being served, even when others fall short."

The Elite 1% knows this to be the most critical step, so they create the opposite effect. After bonding with gratitude, clearly educating them with trust, they swing all their focus into relieving the prospect of any worry. From that point forward, all is well with their world. It has to be easy.

After the prospect has *justified* their action in the education phase, they need to feel relief, knowing that with the trust given to you comes ease of business. It has to be delivered and executed with care, knowing that this, in the end, is what they want the most.

Ease of business is what makes it all worthwhile.

Summary of the Promises and the Importance of Their Order

We went back and experimented several times with the order of the Promises as presented by the world's best. We did everything possible to see if there was another way. We wanted to know if it was luck or was their truth behind their magical sequence. So we went back to the Elite 1% and presented alternative orders of the process and across the board, they dismissed it. They weren't even willing to experiment and try to do it differently. They knew it was a specific order for a reason, and they proved it to us by easily predicting the results if they were ever taken out of sequence.

1. Gratification
2. Education
3. Ease of business

It has to be in that order with no exception.

By now, we had grown to believe in these folks and knew that whatever they told us was true, but in the end, science has a passion of its own, and proof needed to be obtained through the familiar path of evidence and reasoning. So, since the Elite 1% were not willing to try, we decided to run the test with those who were considered great marketers, though not in the world's Elite 1%.

It was in these trials that we were struck by a revelation so far outside the box that it almost made everything seem too simplistic, nearly setting us back in our search for proof. As we began to test and retest on the second-tier sales and marketing teams, a story from my past came back to me and finally made sense in and of itself.

Several years ago, when my life was simpler in a BC (Before Children) era, I set a goal of winning my golf club's coveted "most improved player" award of the year. I committed to the work as well as the time, training, and lessons necessary to improve my game. So, after studying the path to success and becoming laser-focused on my commitment, I went to our club pro and made my intentions known. I was excited and ready for the club's coveted prize. Then it all went away when he told me the undeniable truth.

I remember his words like it was yesterday. Clear, concise, and cogent, he never hesitated to embrace my emotion when he simply said, "It will never happen, kid."

"What!" I exclaimed. "You obviously don't know how hard I am willing to work."

He was gracious as he pulled up my handicap records, studying them, and he began to explain.

"I see you are an 18 handicap," he said. "That's solid and in line with the rest of the world."

"Yeah, but I want to get that down to a 7 or 8 —maybe even a 5."

"That's awesome and certainly a great goal that I know you'll achieve. I have seen you on the range, and I feel we can get you there with some commitment and little hard work."

With the abrupt switch to praise, I was a bit confused.

"Shouldn't that get me the most improved award?" I said. "Who could possibly move farther up the ranks than an 18 handicap who works hard and gets down to a 5?"

"Well," he said, smiling, "that's not exactly how it works. You see, with hard work you can certainly hit your goals, but doing so doesn't make you the most improved player. That belongs to an elite group, and you are just not there yet."

My own curiosity was summoned to pick my bruised ego up off the floor. I needed it to stuff by bruises safely in a pocket somewhere in my heart. As much as I hated to hear those words, it was interesting, and I wanted to understand more.

The club pro continued, "The most improved is not the 18 who gets to a 5, but the 2 that gets to a 1 or a 1 handicap who gets to a scratch."

It's in the elite circles where improvement becomes truly difficult, not in the ranks of the novice. It is so much harder for an elite player to improve by a single stroke than it is for a weekend club player to practice a little and shave down his handicap with a few successful rounds.

"That should never take you away from your goals," he told me, "and maybe in a few years when you get closer to that elite status, you'll understand." Simply put, "The better you are, the harder it gets to improve."

It sounded right, but I must admit that I would not realize how truthful he was until we began to study the Perfect Plan and the best of the best.

This is why the Elite 1% didn't want to change up the order. They knew it worked, and to them it was fundamental, untouchable. So why mess with something that wasn't broken? Once we knew their commitment to success and understood the handicap system of golf and life, we had no problem experimenting with the order but had to move outside the Elite 1% and over to the top 10% who were willing to try. We moved outside the Elite 1%, because they simply knew better and wanted to leave it alone. You just don't mess with science, even if you have to prove it to yourself.

When we experimented with the order, we decided to focus on the traditional apex of those recognized as top achievers by their respected fields, but not quite in the Elite 1% range. We looked toward the bell curve of corporate navigation, to use those nestled in the top 20%, and were willing to attempt things differently. They, the top 20%, were encouraged to participate in an event out-of-order from the Perfect Plan and were asked to build on relationships differently than those in the 1% tier.

The group was wonderful and eager (a lot like me with the golf lessons), and they allowed us to document and tweak the experiment as we shifted the order and asked for their patience. It was grand and we were thrilled, but in the end, just as we expected. It was a disaster.

Fortunately, what we learned and were able to ultimately prove with facts and emotion was that:

The Perfect Plan absolutely has to be presented in the proper order: Gratification, Education, and Ease of Business.

Bonding through the emotion of gratitude, explaining the facts, and then closing the loop with the emotion of relief — this is how the Elite 1% *always* do it.

It's almost like a hamburger, if you can visualize it. The emotions are the two buns, and the meat is the facts. You sandwich the facts between the emotions, knowing that they will most likely forget most of the details in the middle, but trust that *you* know them … and that's good enough for them.

If they know you are grateful, they in turn will be thankful that they are with you and that you have made it easy. Then, and only then, will they respond and follow you.

The top bun — Gratification — is an Emotion of Bonding that leads to 100% recall

The meat of the burger — Education — represents the Facts that only 6% can recall but build a Trust that you are the expert.

The bottom bun is Ease of Business and had an emotional recall of 100%. It works and the process is delicious.

You see, it's not enough to *sell or lead* someone. People knowingly or unknowingly prefer to be with people who share a common belief system. They want to work with people who they feel they *know* and *trust.*

The order of the Perfect Plan's three promises is pure in the most logical way. It establishes the bond, delivers the facts, and relieves the person with an easier way of doing business. *The order is Perfect* in itself, but there is more to it.

Today, anyone could create a TV commercial or an advertising layout using Gratification, Education, and Ease of Business. It is simple enough and would get some significant results from the marketing trackers and rating agencies, but that is not enough.

The missing element, the reason that not just anyone can do it, is the human connection. It is the genuine person-to-person interaction that builds trust and the feeling, "I want to be around this person."

Watching a TV commercial doesn't answer the question of *who* you are or *what* you believe. Knowing what you believe is essential to the trust process. People always want to be with and do business with those whom they feel are on the same page. That's what drives us into the next stage of the Perfect Plan: The Beliefs.

Chapter 8 – The Beliefs Systems of the Perfect Plan

Now we come to the Beliefs.

When the Three Promises of the Perfect Plan collide with the Three Beliefs of the Plan, you have given the prospect, and those you lead, everything they require to answer the following questions:

1. Is this right for me personally?
2. Is this right for me professionally?
3. Is this right for me spiritually (in my conscience)?

Harmony can only exist in one's life when these three questions can be answered unanimously affirmative. Until a person can emphatically say "yes!" to all three questions, they are in disarray and conflict. Only when the collision occurs between Promises and Beliefs, and peace settles on the decision-maker, can clarity and understanding prevail. When it does, and the answer to each of the questions become clear and in line, that's when the magic happens.

Remember, a person will always recall how he or she felt when with you, so your Beliefs must shine forth. This is where they connect and affirm your work and their future success.

It goes without saying that when it comes to belief systems, everyone and every culture is unique. There are a *lot* of different systems that propel people forward in life. Some are based on hard work, others focus on critical thought, but seldom does anyone stop and ask the question, "Who are you?"

One of the amazing facts found in the Perfect Plan is centered on the actual *individual*. The three Promises are unique and can be taught, but there is another variable that brings it all together and is based on *who* the Elite 1% are as a *people*. They are groups who, like many others, have a belief system that varies from person to person and culture to culture.

In our research, we found at least 20 different broad-based beliefs made up the *who* of the Elite 1%, but there were three standout beliefs that existed in all of them. Regardless of where they were in the world, 100% have them in common. These three Beliefs were so prominent that once we realized their existence, it became obvious that they were the key that made these folks so great.

Our team's "Ah-ha!" moment came one day when we realized that the same formula used on the Promise side of the equation existed in equal proportion with their Beliefs. Just as the Promises worked in an order that bonded with emotion, followed by the facts, and sealed with emotion, so did the Beliefs. The emotion/facts/emotion grid reigned true with the Beliefs as well! In fact, they carried the same logic and profound wisdom. However, where the Promises were a statement of what the Top 1% *did* for the prospect, the Beliefs were a revelation of *who* the Top 1% were at heart.

These three beliefs make up the collision point between the Promises of the Perfect Plan and the understanding of *who* you are.

Gratification (Emotion) collides with → #1

Education (Facts) collides with → #2

Ease of Business (Emotion) collides with → #3

Belief #1 – Create, Don't Compete

Everyone would agree that there is something special about a creative person. You might also agree that after painting a room or doing anything artistic, a person feels a profound sense of accomplishment unique and unlike any other emotion. The emotion created when someone is in the act of being creative, or just the observance of someone else's creativity, is staggering and eerily attractive.

When we studied the vast variety of emotions that a person might feel or express on any given day, we noticed a parallel between the bonding action of Gratitude and the stimulation of positive emotion rooted in creativity.

As we dug deeper, we found an equal neurological energy that is emitted when stimulation is felt from the emotion of Creativity. This is in complete agreement with the studies conducted at University of North Carolina at Chapel Hill about couples bonding for 60 or more years via Gratification. It was not just the bond of creativity, but the stimulation of creativity that kept them magnetized for so long.

We once believed that Creativity was only an isolated act or a physical motion, i.e. the *action* of creation, but we quickly discovered that Creativity is an *emotion* as well, falling into the same category as Gratitude. A person can easily express Gratitude by physical works and deeds, but the acceptance or receipt of Gratitude is 100% emotional. The same is true for Creativity. It can be a physical action, but to be *part of* the actual Creativity requires the act to morph into an emotion.

It is a very special transformation. We discovered that, much like Gratification, Creativity is a magnetizing emotion based on stimulation. **When someone senses another person's Creativity, they become magnetized by it and are stimulated to be with or around them.**

The Elite 1% knows this all too well.

The other side of the coin is that most leadership, sales and marketing folks focus, as you guessed, on the wrong action. Instead of *creating*, they focus on *competing*, and this is erroneous in the eyes of the elite who believe that their job with the client is to create, not compete.

74

Competition is a big word in a variety of different ways, and if you study it, it is possible to get lost in its origins and meaning. Its English roots translate to "an act striving for supremacy between static performers." Thus, if you are competing, you are the same as your opponent — static, or simply average.

In a way, today's culture seems to embrace competition, but for all the wrong reasons. One of the sidebar studies we completed within the Perfect Plan centered on the concept that true competition would result in an equal distribution of win/losses. In other words, when everyone is the same – i.e., static or average – the win/loss ratio should come remarkably close to 50/50 every time.

The exception landed in what broke the mold for the Elite 1%. No one prior to our study, to the best of our knowledge, had ever asked: Why do they reign supreme in their fields? In our quest for an answer, we studied major league and professional sports that spread their season over several months and played more than 25 games. Within the U.S., it came down to Major League Baseball and professional basketball (the NBA), and what we discovered was fascinating.

When competition is at such an elite level as the NBA or MLB, talent was the key to most wins and losses. Talent was also the variable that got most of the teams into the postseason, but it was not what made them champions. As we studied deeper and opened our minds to a new and fresh approach, it became clear how little the players had to do with championship wins.

Players, by their very nature, tend to float between teams. Some are traded by the team owners, others are hurt or renew contracts with other teams, and many simply bounce from team to team trying to find a home. As we studied the numbers, we found that championship teams, especially dynasty teams that are known for their multiple, repeat championships, retain only 55% of their players from one championship year to another. In stark contrast, close to 100% retained their coaches. In other words, the coaches became the only reliable variable in the study of championship teams, and that lead us to understand that it is not the players and the talent who win the championships, it is the *coaches.*

If you look back at the greatest coaches of all time, most had multiple championship wins with different teams and talent: Joe Torre (Atlanta Braves, New York Yankees, L.A. Dodgers), Tony La Russa (Oakland A's, St. Louis Cardinals), Phil Jackson (Chicago

Bulls, L.A. Lakers), John Wooden (Indiana State, UCLA – 10 championships in 12 years with different players!), Nick Saban (LSU, Alabama). The list goes on and on.

So why do coaches win championships and players don't?

It's all about creativity.

Coaches have the ability to make chess moves within a game, to orchestrate a result by creatively using the talent and tools available. Coaches can call timeouts, substitute players, call plays, and much more. They execute teamwork with their leadership and use their Creativity to see beyond the field of play. Like the Elite 1%, the *talent* of their product and team was superb, but it was their Creativity that defines them. No one can deny that the marketplace is full of others trying to competitively bump you off your perch. They want to fight for the same client and get in the game with you, but the belief system of the Elite 1% allows them to forgo any thoughts of competition. The best-of-the-best never want to be the same as the rest. They are different, and they magnetize people to them with their Creativity, not by competitive flair.

They are not there to compete for the client's business at all. They never thought about competition. They never wanted to be anywhere near such a concept.

I like to talk about this when we do our Deep Dive training sessions. The word "competition" comes from Greek, Latin, and old English root words that mean "static" or "the same." So think about this: When someone says, "I am competitive" or "I am competing," they are saying, "I am the same as everyone else."

On the contrary, we found it to be a universal belief that people want to be around those who are creative and innovative, not those who are competitive. No one wants to follow someone who is static, the same as everyone else, much less someone who is average. If you believe the test results and understand that in competition, anyone can beat anyone else on any given day, then the odds are quite … boring.

People don't want to pay for boring. They want something special.

People want attraction, and they are stimulated to those who, in their very body, soul, and spirit, are creative.

The Elite 1% established their Creativity immediately. It is the foundation of their belief system, and they can move faster than anyone else. They universally deny competition and project an attitude that reveals, "I am here to create and I am a creative person."

Another, not-so-scientific means of proving this point is cable titan, The Food Network. This is a great organization that is changing the way the Western world looks at food by making it fun again. In a meeting, I asked how many in the audience had ever seen The Food Network on TV. About 80% of them raised their hands — the other 20% were no doubt lying.

I then asked how many of them had attempted to make any of the food demonstrated on the network. Less than 15% indicated that they had. That is an interesting discovery.

Here's the point: The Food Network isn't banking its success on their viewers actually *duplicating* what their chefs make. They know that what attracts you to their channel is the fact that their chefs are engaged in the act of *creating.* This is the magnetizing emotion — the stimulation — that they want to create within you. This is reason so many late-night viewers will be hypnotized to watch the show at 2 in the morning. There is an undeniable attraction to art of creation. This is why we are willing to watch talented chefs take raw materials and make something glorious from them. Think about it. The Cupcake Wars? How can they make a successful show around *cupcakes?* Easy — it's the creation. It's the innovation. It's the stimulation and magnetism that pulls you into their show.

It is the mindset of creation and the act of being creative that is important to the Elite 1%. It is not selling a product or leading the masses, it is about the art of drawing them in.

Create. Don't compete.

Gratification (Emotion) =

Create! Don't Compete (Emotion)

Belief #2 – Exceed Expectations at All Times

The second Belief the elite convey is that the value of what they are offering is always greater than the cost of that product or service. This is accomplished by exceeding expectations at all times. From delivery to mindset, their focus is on the "wow" factor of their work. They strive for the moment those they lead (or the prospect at hand) stands amazed at the over-delivery of their trust and services.

Once a bond of trust is established with a client, they become clearly educated and establish that this action or deed will make their lives easier. They seek to know you're creative and on top of the situation. This is where you reveal to them that the value of your request is greater than the cost and efforts of their response, therefore you exceed their expectations and the "wow" moment occurs.

Remember, every time you use a number in a speech, email, request, or conversation, you lose half of your audience. It is a dangerous ground to tread, yet we seem compelled to do it every day. The reality is people don't like numbers – even when technical expertise is required.

Most people have preconceived ideas of value and how to measure it. This thought process creates a conflict in their minds between the need for quantitative reality and the fight to avoid the numbers. In the case of "exceeding expectations," if you tell them how much something costs, you are establishing the value through the numbers. This falls short of the belief system because you create perceptions without sharing your belief in its greater value. In doing so, you will lose those who automatically fear the cost is greater than the value. This is not what you want.

Buyers today are conditioned to believe that numbers are never valid or sincere. The adulteration of data over the years to fit whatever scenario is required has made the general public suspicious. Mark Twain, the great American writer, was credited with declaring there are three types of liars — "liars, damn liars, and statisticians." He summed it up well.

We know as we look back on Promise 2 (Education), English-speaking buyers can comprehend only three topics at a time, and most other cultures are the same. This comes from the way we sequence numbers in our mind, and with the English language,

78

speakers are in a terrible position before they ever get out of the gate.

Let me give you an example. With the English language, we count 1 to 10 with no issue, and then, without rhyme or reason, we develop the numbers 11 and 12. What is strange here is that these two numbers break the total logic of the sequence in their *word form* (eleven and twelve). There is no sound or root meaning that assigns a number 1 and 2 to the Ten to create the eleven and twelve — it just appears out of logical developmental order.

But never worry. The English language gets back on track with the teens. *Thirteen* is really 3 plus 10 — expressed 'thir' (three) and 'teen' (ten). Then 4 and 10 for *fourteen*, and 5 and 10 for *fifteen* and so on, all the way to 20, or 2 tens.

The English sequence of numbers, with the exception of 11 and 2, makes perfect sense on its way to the number 20, but just to make life difficult, that's when the language flips the order. Instead of continuing the same sequence of sounds —logically putting the one in front of the 2 tens (twenty) — we flip the sequence of sounds and say *twenty-one* or 2 tens and 1.

By flipping the order without reason, the exact opposite of the sound patterns we used prior in the teens occurs.

Once again in English, the first 21 numeric sequences between the number 1 and 21 actually changes the logic of how the language sequences the sound patterns four times. No wonder people are afraid of numbers! This dramatically illogical changing of patterns and sequences contributes to why English-speaking kids seem to struggle with basic mathematics, especially fractions.

To top it off and make it more confusing, between the illogical combinations of the language patterns and sounds, we throw another curve ball and start to break down the trailing possessives into 'st,' 'nd,' 'rd,' and 'th' (1st, 2nd, 3rd, and 4th). This really creates a problem.

The result is clear. English-speaking humans, whether buyers, consumers or team members you want to lead, have trouble with numbers when they become too complex, and unfortunately that occurs before they get to the number 21. What people really want and need in today's world is a *trusted advisor* to help them understand that the *value* is not in the *number* but in the result. They also need help *feeling* the outcome really is greater than the price —

or, put another way, you have exceeded their expectations and prove it to be true. It doesn't matter if the cost is something they pay, you pay, or someone else pays for, they just want to know if the value they are getting is really there, even if they have trouble understanding the numbers.

This is why it is so important that they trust you. If they trust you, then your Belief in the *value* will be another bonding agent that becomes the emotional response they base their decision upon. In Promise 2 (Education), we taught you that people will remember only 6% of what you say. This is because they want to outsource their success to you and they want to know that *you* are the expert, that *you* are confident, and that *you* are sincere. It is the same with this belief component — if you continue to build on confidence and trust by simply stating your personal belief that the value is greater than the cost, the next step in the Perfect Plan will accelerate you toward a favorable conclusion.

The "value is greater than the cost" will be the fuel that creates an environment where you "exceed their expectations" at all times.

Gratification (Emotion) -------------Create! Don't Compete. (Emotion)

Education (Facts)--------------------Exceed Expectations At All Times (Facts)

Ease of Business (Emotion)---------Belief #3

Belief #3 – Give Forward Without Any Expectation of Anything in Return

The third Belief we discovered within those who make up the Top 1% is something that, quite frankly, astounded us. For the first eight years of our research, we had this phenomenon worded incorrectly in our research. It was based on cultural acceptance of the actions usually associated with the belief, but no one seemed to dig deeper and ask, "Why?" Nevertheless, it revealed itself to be the core fabric that weaves throughout their entire belief system. No matter who the best are leading, or what they were trying to sell, do, or achieve, in

---

the end, they were all the same — they never *gave back*, they only *gave forward.*

They gave forward without any expectation of anything in return.

At first, we had misworded this belief under the title of *Giving Back*, but soon we came to learn that this wasn't true. The Elite 1% never gave back. Their mindset was much more advanced. They avoided the cultural dance created to manipulate people by leveraging a concept that "you are privileged so you must give to those who are not as fortunate." It was fueled by a tit-for-tat concept founded upon the logic of "if you give me something, I'll give you something in return." This is the societal norm used to drive much of today's charitable giving by creating an inherent premeditated guilt consciousness based on the conceptual tagline we all need to give back, but once again, this is where the English language fails us.

The term "giving back" implies that something was "taken," and this is where the guilty feeling associated with many social charities drive their mission. They are, in their own way, violating the Perfect Plan by using emotions to create unwanted feeling, thus coupling guilt as the antidote and them as the benefactors.

Fortunately, the Elite 1% sees through this game and stand above it all. They know that charity is not an elaborate guilt offering designed to cleanse you from the sin of your good fortune, but charity is an act of joyful love sharing the things you have been asked to steward. When this mindset steps in and erases society's attempt for gain, a level of enlightenment occurs that few understand.

For the Elite 1%, it is a pleasure and a joy to give, but they never give back, they only give forward.

There was never an obligation or contract — explicit or implied — in the mind of the elite. There was never any condition or expectation, guilt or sin. They gave unconditionally.

They simply gave forward, and they did so without any expectation of anything in return.

This is meant exactly as it is written. The best-of-the-best were not concerned with getting anything back for themselves. That wasn't what was important to them. They didn't feel obligated nor did they feel the need to cleanse themselves of any guilt associated with their unique path in life. Giving Forward is a belief that reveals who these people really are — stewards of a gift.

Additionally, those who give forward don't mind sharing their work or telling the world what they are doing for others. The Western concept of "anonymous giving" is great, but it weakens the opportunity to motivate others to do the same. When the Elite 1% has the opportunity to share, they do. For example, when they approach someone and want to motivate them to become generous givers themselves, they have no problem saying, "Here's what we are doing for the community and for you. We want you to have it." If you are uncomfortable with the idea or think it to be bragging a bit, then don't, because they give forward anyway. Most people would be shocked at how often opportunities present themselves to give, and the best always did it without question and without an alternate agenda.

The Elite 1% from around the world, from every culture and language, all shared this core Belief. They are — across the board — generous, giving people who do so without any expectation of anything in return. When someone is giving for the right reasons, people pick up on it. It makes the Top 1% highly attractive and trustworthy. There is a special aura and glow about them. To give and have no intention of looking for a reward or to make a sale is unique and special in today's world, regardless of where you live and the language you speak.

Giving comes in all shapes and sizes. It can be in the form of time, talent, or treasure. It can be physical, a presence that is there when needed, and it can be labor on behalf of another. One of my favorite stories of giving came from one of the Elite 1% while telling me how someone had made an impact on him in his early years.

Danny Strickland was a young, eager college graduate who wanted to take on the world. He was the first in his family to attend and graduate from college, having grown up, as he puts it, on "the wrong side of the tracks in a town already poor and beaten down."

He was lucky, and knew it. Through a series of fortunate events, hard work, and commitment, Danny made it out of that small town and graduated from an elite Northern school with a degree in chemistry. It was 1970, and he was instantly in demand. The space race was in full throttle and the Cold War loomed in the back of everyone's mind. Upon graduation, Danny was immediately offered a job at one of the nation's leading firms, Procter & Gamble. He jumped on it.

Aspiring to change the world, he envisioned himself working on top secret projects for the military and, hopefully, working with astronauts and NASA's finest engineers. Danny knew something great lay ahead for him, and this opportunity seemed to line up perfectly with his plan to make an impact on the world around him. He knew he had made it when he was asked to accept a promotion and take over a new project for P&G as a Technical Brand Manager! Without hesitation or even asking what the job entailed, he jumped at the opportunity and committed to being the best young manager they had to offer.

"What could it be?" he thought to himself. "Maybe something to do with fighting the Soviets or, better yet, something that would take me to the White House to meet the President."

The anticipation almost killed him before he ever set foot into his new office or met his new team.

The next morning, he woke up early and with his energy level at full throttle, Danny practically ran to the P&G headquarters to get his new assignment and his first crack at something big.

He arrived eager to take on the world and was shocked when they gave him his assignment.

At first, he refused to believe what he had heard. Had they really said that? Did they really want him to do *that?*

Yes, they did.

His mind fought to process the moment. What do those words mean?

"Laundry detergent?"

He echoed in disbelief.

After a moment of dazed incoherence and confusion, the words rang in his head like Sunday Church bells.

"Laundry detergent?" he repeated, dumbfounded.

"Yes," they said. "Welcome to 'Big Soap.' "

Little did Danny know what he was given at the time, but this was a huge part of Procter & Gamble's revenue.

"Big Soap," as they called it, made up over 50% of Procter and Gamble's revenue, and it was something that everyone used. The market was literally endless. However, to Danny, it was not about what it *was*, it was more about what it *was not*. As he saw it, it was not astronauts, nor was it a cool new James Bond-like spy chemical, and worst of all, it would most likely not get him any invitations to the White House.

What it ended up being was a *start* to something great. He just could not see it at the time.

On his first day with his new team (i.e., one analyst and a part-time secretary), Danny had the pleasure of meeting someone who, looking back on it years later, was part of the Elite 1% himself. Bob Hall was his name, and in 1971, he was someone who saw the world in a different light than most people could imagine. Bob, without ever knowing it, was about to start a chain effect that would change the world by giving forward.

When he first approached Danny, it seemed a bit consolatory, like a big brother comforting his younger sibling because he did not make the varsity team. What was to happen next was one of those "wow" moments that changes a person's life in a profound way.

As they sat together, Bob began to share some of his wisdom with Danny that was rich in *good* advice, *good* understanding, and *good* news. Bob knew that Danny was disappointed in the unforeseen turn in the road of life that now was taking him to Big Soap. As Bob sat with Danny that day, he told him something that, in his own words, "will change *your* life forever."

Yes, you read that correctly — *your life ... you who are reading these words.* It certainly changed Danny's life.

Bob gave Danny a challenge that sounded so simple that the impact of those words will resonate with Danny for the next 40 years.

Bob told him, "If you want to change the world and make a big impact, you have to make a decision and decide if you want to help people improve the quality of their lives."

"Of course I do," Danny said. "But I'm working on soap ... laundry detergent, to be exact."

Bob smiled and continued, "You see, Danny, the decision you need to make is not about *if you want to impact their lives*, but *how you are going to do it*. How do you want to affect the quality of their lives?"

Perplexed, Danny listened as Bob went on to explain, "You come to a point where you have to decide. To change the world, you will either do something big for a very few people, or something small for a large number of people." He paused and fixed Danny with a gentle but serious look. "So, decide today — what do you want to do?"

"Do you want to do a little for a lot, or a lot for a little?"

Knowing that Danny was absorbing the advice, he went on to help him understand the concept a little bit further. He told him about the type of impact you can have on the lives of people that comes with no glory or awards but affects people beyond their own imagination. He pointed out that everyone around Danny wore clothes that they had to clean every day. "That's the 'a lot' part," he said.

So, if everyone you see is doing something similar, and you can make a small impact in that area that affects the quality of his or her life for the better, then you can change the world! Even if it is just laundry soap.

"So," he concluded, "why don't you come up with a way to make their clothes brighter and cleaner faster than we do it today? Make it quicker."

"Imagine what it would it be like if you could affect their lives in the smallest way, but in turn, everyone gets a little bit ahead?"

Danny found, in Bob's giving forward of his wisdom via *good* advice, those words would lead to *good* understanding, and ultimately changed the world with *good* news.

Danny went on to apply Bob's wisdom, and what began as a mundane project to take phosphates out of detergent and ended up changing the world for a lot of people within an icon — Tide Detergent. From there, Danny never stopped applying the principles Bob taught him that day, and he went on to work on Era, Downy, Gain, Oxydol, Ivory Soap and Drift. He literally changed the world for a *lot* of people in a very small way, and only a select few knew it.

A few years later, Danny got the call he had been waiting for. It was time for a new project. He felt great about what he had accomplished and was finally ready for the limelight. Then it happened again. Danny was so good at what he did that they wanted him to start a new division to make the world a better place, but guess what?

As Danny likes to say, grinning ear to ear, "What could possibly be less sexy than detergent?

How about diapers ... *adult* diapers!"

Danny almost passed out. He could not believe what he heard. His big promotion leads him to the world of adult diapers, but that's when the drive and determination to change the world kicked in. He took on the job with a passion to change the world once again.

As he began to think through the market potential of this new idea (adult diapers), he began to see the true need that existed in the market. He often thought back on Bob's wisdom and began to try to find a way to affect people's lives, even without the glory or fame.

Soon, Danny learned that the No. 1 reason people were entering nursing homes at the time was for incontinence. The social stigma and lack of adequate care had created an open door for perfectly productive people to enter unproductive nursing homes — all because of the social embarrassment associated with incontinence. That's when Danny decided he would change the world for a lot of people yet again, but in a very small way. He threw himself into his work and focused on the opportunity to help others in ways no one had before. In the end, he did it, and it changed lives.

To this day, Danny gets teary-eyed just talking about it. "You would have never believed it, but for the first time in modern history, people began to *leave* nursing homes to resume their lives and become happy and productive in society once again." He remembers receiving letters of sincere gratitude from people all around the world he never met but who thanked him for saving their lives.

He did it. A little change, for a lot of people, made the world a better place.

All of this because of his personal belief to give forward without any expectation of anything in return, and the wisdom Bob Hall gave him some 40 years ago.

The product? Depends Adult Diapers.

From there, Danny finally did realize his dreams, but he never forgot what Bob had taught him. He repeated that advice over and over in a career that took him to become an impactful leader of the several of the world's largest consumer goods companies, both in the U.S. and in Europe.

—

When Danny officially retired, he had made it. As the No. 2 guy at Coca Cola in charge of all product innovation and brands, he had made impact after impact on the world. From juice to sports drinks, and even bottled water, Danny was there. He literally changed the world, all because another of the Elite 1% gave forward with time and talent all those years ago.

As of this writing, Danny still gives forward. His foundation has funded schools and scholarships to help people who will never know who is impacting them or why, but he, as an Elite 1% member himself, he still remembers the words from Bob and never ceases to give forward.

A little for a lot, or a lot for a little.

Either way, you affect the quality of people's lives, and you *give forward*.

Gratification (Emotion) ----------→Create! Don't Compete. (Emotion)

Education (Facts)------------------→The Value is Greater Than the Cost (Facts)

Ease of Business (Emotion)------→Give Forward (Emotion)

Chapter 9 – Bringing it All Together

Getting inside the Mind of the Decision-Maker with the Perfect Plan.

Like anything else, people need assurance before they make a decision. For many, following a designated path or spending hard-earned money can be a fearful thing. You, like those you serve, know that people want something in return for their investment that outweighs the actual cost of the item or service.

People want value.

Before they make such a commitment, they want to trust the individual who will shepherd the deal. When you add Gratification, Education, and Ease of Business, you create the basis for establishing trust with your client or prospect.

In the case of the world's Elite 1%, they begin by establishing themselves with a sincere bond. Once the bond is established with an Attitude of Gratitude, they clearly educated, and lives were made easier. Then, as they share their belief systems, they were there to create, not to compete. They knew that the value of what they were offering exceeded the cost and made certain to share it. They wanted to give forward without any expectation of return.

We have learned that people remember 100% of how they felt when they were with you but recall just 6% of what you said. This sets the foundation for the patterns and logic on both sides of the Promises and the Beliefs, and it is based on the sincerity of the one leading and presenting a solution.

Think about it with this simple chart:

The Promises	The Beliefs
Gratification Emotion = 100% recall	Create, Don't Compete Emotion = 100% recall
Education Facts = 6% recall	Exceed Expectations Facts = 6% recall
Ease of Business Emotion = 100% recall	Always Give Forward Emotion = 100% recall

When the Three Promises collide with the Three Beliefs, you have a magical moment. It is something amazing to witness. When you see it, you can't help but to exclaim, "Wow!"

Here is the incredible part. This entire belief system is powered by something that every Elite 1% leader, sales and marketing person knows to be true! They know, at the moment the presentation ends, when the perfect order of Promises is supported by the perfect order of Beliefs — in a collision together — the decision-maker who just witnessed the event will make a decision based on their ability to answer three simple questions:

1. Is this right for me personally?
2. Is this right for me professionally?
3. Is this right for me spiritually (in my conscience)?

Gratification (Emotion)-----> <-------Create! Don't Compete. (Emotion)

Education (Facts)------> <-------The Value is Greater Than the Cost (Facts)

Ease of Business (Emotion)----> <-----Give Forward (Emotion)

⇩

Is this right for me personally?

Is this right for me professionally?

Is this right for me spiritually (in my conscience)?

Every consumer, decision-maker, parent, student, couple, and critical thinker will ultimately ask themselves these questions before they make their decision final. The best of the best know that the answers have to be an *affirmative* to all three questions, because only then can there be harmony in the decision-maker's mind.

Only then can there be a Good Decision.

Only then can there be a Wise Decision.

All three areas, Personal, Professional, and Spiritual, must align or there is no deal.

Even though some will push and pull to try to make a marginal call on one of the three, it never works for them. All three areas must be made 100% in confidence and each must stand alone. Once they do, the decision is viewed as perfect and harmonious.

The best of the best know this, but in their elite way of thinking they answer these questions for the client in their own mind before their process ever begins. The Elite 1%, in their own way, will give forward in an effort to make sure that the answers to these questions are "yes!"

When the Elite 1% believes the client can answer "yes" to all of these questions, the presentation begins.

This is Good News.

With this discovery of logic — that the elite actually look ahead to ensure their actions are in the client's best interest — everything began to turn upside down for our team.

This is where we began to see it clearly.

It was almost a heart-stopping moment, much like watching a great mystery movie and you realize the character you thought was the bad guy wasn't. In our case, they were never bad guys, but the transformation was astonishing. Our consideration of these folks turned from the good, to the better, to the perfect.

You see, this is where we came to our own conclusion, before we realized that we were potentially looking down the wrong scientific path.

To discover how the Elite 1% of the world's leaders, sales and marketing teams performed, we found a revelation within the Perfect Plan. The men and women we had determined were the best leadership, sales and marketing professionals in the world *didn't consider themselves to be in leadership, sales and marketing!*

What?

It was true.

Had we made the most colossal error in science?

Did we really forget to ask them *who* they were?

Did we forget to ask those in the elite class what they did for a living?

With all humility and grace, it was true. As we studied the Elite 1% of performers in a global search for the truth, we made an error and assumed we knew what they did for a living.

We assumed that the largest dairy manufacturing facilities in Italy were in the dairy business.

We assumed that the largest tortilla factory in Monterey, Mexico made tortillas.

We assumed that the cell phone distributors in Eastern Europe sold cell phones.

We assumed, assumed, and assumed again.

After the shock wore off and the grand realization of our failure settled in our minds, we buckled up and went back to work. This time, we started off properly and began to ask each of the subjects, those classified as the Elite 1% in their field, "What is it that you do for a living?"

What happened next astounded us, and brought everything together with a divine wind.

While the answers should have been apparent, as we thought they would be, the Elite 1% shocked us once again.

Their answers, no matter what action they lead or skill they acquired, no matter what product they sold, were all the same.

Test Subject 1: What do you do for a living?

I serve others.

Test Subject 2: What do you do for a living?

I serve others.

Test Subject 3: What do you do for a living?

I serve others.

Test Subject 4: What do you do for a living?

I serve others.

Test Subject 5: What do you do for a living?

I serve others.

And so on and so on...

To our amazement, they didn't believe that they were leadership, sales or marketing, nor did they ever refer to themselves as such. For all those years, the secret key to their success remained hidden from us until that very moment. For a fleeting second, we had a momentary panic as we saw the entire project flash before our eyes.

How did we miss something so big?

It was a strange sensation at first, but then we realized what had happened. We had *good* advice, we found *good* understanding, but now ... above all ... we finally received our *good* news.

What we learned was their secret.

We now knew what made them special and it warmed our hearts and challenged our very being.

You see, the Elite 1% are who they are because they don't see what they do for a living as an opportunity to be a leader or sell a product.

They see it as an opportunity to *serve!*

That was it. That was the missing link!

The pattern was Perfect — we knew that much.

A series of three perfectly aligned Promises that formed a bond of Gratitude they would never forget, created clear Education and trust in the presenter's expertise, followed by an unforgettable and relieving emotion of Ease of Business.

Why?

Because that is what servants do!

Then, the Promises were met by a Perfect Belief system of *who* the presenter was and what he believed. They were magnetizing with creativity yet never competed. The value was greater than the price, and above all, they gave forward ... without any expectation of anything in return.

Why?

Because that is what servants do!

When they were done, the prospect or decision- maker would consciously and subconsciously ask themselves three questions:

1. Is this right for me personally?
2. Is this right for me professionally?
3. Is this right for me spiritually (in my conscience)?

If the answer was yes for all three, then a harmony exists and they knew the decision to be made was good and Perfect. The Elite 1%, however, took it one more step further. This is where the light turned on, and we understood why what they did was always *good* news.

The Elite 1% never starts with the Promises and Beliefs. That is actually where they end.

They accomplish great things as a servant leader by first asking themselves if *they* (the elite) believe the prospect can answer the three questions with a yes. If so, that's where they would start.

Why?

Because that is what *servants* do.

They understood something that was a world changer for us. Many of the Elite 1% have since explained to me that we live in a world where most people confuse the words "service" and "process." Many of those who say they are in the "service business" (i.e., financial services, food services, and even medical services) are not in the service business at all. They are in the "processing business."

Process people move items (and people) from A to B, from one place to another. They become drones, and their customers just flow through their turnstiles, looking for the next process to ride. But for those who understand the *good news* of the Perfect Plan, process is not what they do. They serve others as *servants*.

When we discovered this truth, it changed the dynamics of everything we had learned. It was a moment I will never forget. We discovered that:

The difference in the service business and the process business was not in the procedures, but in those executing the deal.

They taught us that to truly be in the service business, you yourself had to be a servant.

In order to serve, you have to humble yourself to where you can actually *be* the servant.

Then and only then will the Perfect Plan make sense.

It is a servant who will ask if the decision is right for those they serve personally, professionally, and in their spirit.

It is a servant who serves with a bonding Attitude of Gratitude.

It is a servant who clearly educates the client.

It is the servant, the leaders, who will carry the burden, not those they serve.

It is a servant who makes lives easier.

Why? Because that is what a servant does.

From there, when asked, "Who are you?" a servant explains, "As a servant, I am here to create and not compete. As a servant, I will always exceed your expectations. As a servant, I will always give forward."

"Why?"

"Because that is what servants do."

Servants anticipate the needs of those they serve. So if I, as your servant, know something is good for you personally, professionally, and spiritually, then I will offer it to you because it benefits you. This is the basis of *all servant leadership*.

Why? Because that is what a servant does.

So the Elite 1% are special because they start at the end.

This is because they aren't in the leadership, sales and marketing business, and to our surprise, they never were. They were always in the *servant business*. They are servants, and that is the key to the success of every individual in the Elite 1%. They seek to make sure that what they offer is good news for the client. They want to benefit the client and serve the client. They never wanted to lead or sell them anything.

This is why the Perfect Plan is so perfect.

Once something is right personally, professionally, and in a person's spirit, then they will pull the trigger on a decision. The Elite 1% already knows the answer to these questions *before* they ever present the deal. The presentation from that point on is to make sure the client sees the truth and does not get distracted or confused with irrelevant thinking. The elite seek to present the service in a pattern that is perfectly suited for them; they then receive you as a servant.

Their presentation is always based on the thinking of, "How can I best serve those we seek to lead?"

"They will need to know how *grateful* and *thankful* I am.

I will *educate* them clearly on the subject.

I will make it *easy* to work and be with me.

I will also weave in *who I really am*, because they want to trust me, not a product or a service.

They want to work with someone with a similar value system, so I will demonstrate how *creative* I am and show them the full *value* of what I am presenting is much more than the cost.

Then they will know that I have already *given forward* on their behalf without the thought of return because I *value* their relationship more than the product or sale."

Honestly, this is not how the traditional world of 'Leadership, Sales and Marketing" train people to think, but it is most certainly how servants think. Be careful now: Don't confuse *true servants* with those who tout that they are in the service business. In actuality, the people who claim to be in the service business are most likely in the process business. They are just processing things from A to B. They process a sale from beginning to end. That is not *service.*

Service can only be delivered by a servant.

A servant is someone who humbles themselves before another and says, "I am here for you." They know that relationships are more important than products and so they have already determined that this is right for the client, serving the client's interests.

Do you see why this entire process just blew our minds? We were looking to see what the Elite 1% of the leadership, sales and marketing professionals did differently, only to discover that they weren't in leadership, sales or marketing.

They were servants.

Their presentation wasn't a pitch to sell something. It was a humbling of them to serve the interests of the client. This made them genuine and sincere. When combined with the proven processes of the Perfect Plan, it became … perfect.

Wow.

The results were off any measurable grid, and that's why no one paid attention to them. Management systems couldn't comprehend it or wrap their heads around it. They figured there had to be a trick or they were just lucky.

As we now know, it wasn't in the *what*. It is always in the *who*!

Who they were is what made a difference.

Over the years, since the Perfect Plan was originally released, we have had countless industry professionals, ask to borrow or even purchase our "data." They do so believing that it is the actual proposals, books, and pitch books that make the sales, but in all truth; it is the way we humble ourselves and show that we are servants that makes the sale.

It is never the materials. It was always the person.

Somebody once asked me, "You really love what you do, don't you?"

I enthusiastically answered, "Yes!"

They then asked, "What are your loves in your life?"

What an interesting question.

I responded, "I've got five loves in my life. I love God, I love my family, I love this great country, I love the NBA (specifically the Atlanta Hawks) and I love my unique path in life — in that order."

That individual looked a bit confused and asked, "Why?"

I said, "Well, it's easy. I am grateful for them, they contribute to my life, and I love them all. The first three obviously take care of themselves. The NBA is just my little vice, but really, when you want to know *who* I am, it's about the people around me and those we serve."

I am fortunate enough to own a company and work with a team of people who want desperately to give you permission to be who you really are and to unlock a key to success that will help you change the world. Yes, we are consultants. Yes, we are in the sales business. Yes, we manufacture products, but as far as I am concerned, we are *really* here to serve, and in the service business, we are who we are … we are *servants!*

I do have those five loves in my life, and I am passionate about telling people about them and the Perfect Plan, but most important of all, I am Grateful and Thankful toward the people I serve.

It was there in the beginning. It was there all along, and now we understand why.

The original hypothesis was too radical to get the attention it deserved, but it was actually proven true through the study.

In the end, it was true.

It was a Perfect Plan.

Chapter 10 – Closing Remarks

Who We Are and What We Believe

For the over 25 years, my team and I have been a leader in the institutional global sales and marketing business. I have been successful while leading great teams and companies to their own success. Some were easier than others, but I stand today honored to have served them all, each to the very best of my ability.

I actually found my way into the world of institutional finance shortly after that night in New Orleans over 25 years ago with my old boss. He encouraged me into institutional finance and global sales because he had always admired the fact that those folks could control their own schedules and impact lives. That sounded good enough for me, so I took his advice and dove into the deep end as fast as I could.

So, I have spent the past quarter of a century serving people via a unique path built on observation and experience. It all started in 1987 and has evolved into some of the world's largest and most desirable companies becoming my clients. Today, they include some of the most recognized international brands, and we have averaged about $1 billion a year in annual sales.

I have changed firms a few times during my career, each move based on personal growth and where I felt my skills were taking me. I never left a firm for any reason other than personal growth. I have been fortunate enough to work for some of the top firms on Wall Street and in the global financial industry. I still have friends at all of them. I even provide complimentary Perfect Plan training for them since, in their own ways, each contributed to the revelation that ultimately began in 2001.

In 2001, I was employed by what I considered to be one of the world's finest organizations, MetLife. It was, and still is, a dynamic little Fortune 100 company that is known for its insurance and financial products as well as their long-running association with Charles Schulz's famous Peanuts characters. During my time there, I become their top institutional sales representative, and my office grew to the point where we made up 27% of their national U.S. production for their RS Division. I also had the pleasure of working with two of world's finest CEOs, Robert "Bob" BenMosche, and C. Robert "Rob" Henrikson. They taught me more than I can give them credit. Bob taught me to take things on with authenticity and vigor,

Rob taught me how to be me. Rob and I spent a lot of evenings driving around the South practicing for what would become, at the time, history's largest IPO. I also had the good fortune of working with some of the best sales management teams and professionals available, especially with MetLife's Vice President of International Sales, Tim Mitchell.

Without knowing it, Tim set the Perfect Plan on its foundation.

Tim can see and understand cultures and personalities better than anyone I have ever known. He is a friend to anyone in the room, and his strategic mind has the ability to understand human behavior at a level that transcends anyone I have ever met. In the fall of 2001, when the U.S. economy was in turmoil and the world was gripped with fear and rage, Tim came to me with an idea that would connect deeply with the work I had already begun for the Perfect Plan a few months prior. His idea would conveniently couple with the Perfect Plan and will one day lead to what I feel will ultimately change the way we communicate, offer our services, and set the policies that regulate world trade.

I was in my office that day when Tim approached me with a proposition that was hidden inside a question. "Do you think there might be a common thread between the world's elite sales people … regardless of what they sell?"

Wow, I thought, what an interesting idea and eerily similar to the "radical" hypothesis I had developed at the beach on July 4th.

I have always believed that there are no coincidences in life, and his timing was perfect. One of my favorite Mark Twain quotes puts it in perspective: "Coincidences are God's way of remaining anonymous."

Tim had both the coolest and most challenging job in the world. He managed a sales force that touched almost every continent, and was responsible for shaping all of them into the MetLife way of doing business. He had to do it by not disrupting the local culture, a task that frequently looked impossible. I was first introduced to Tim at a meeting near Mexico City, and we quickly became friends. I had no idea how lucky I was at the time, because Tim is the kind of person everyone needs to know. He has a beautiful family, four lovely kids, and countless grandchildren, but he also has a lot of class — something you just can't buy or even learn. Tim just has it.

One of the things that made Tim unique is his special way of seeing things in three-dimensional space, a skill that allowed him to understand what really drives behavior. That fall, his simple question evolved into a lot more than a mere lunchtime chat.

Tim had started to recognize that great sales people, all over the world, had similar tendencies, and he asked me if I wanted to take a closer look at them. In hindsight, and after a few lengthy late-night discussions, I now know that the reason he came to me was because not only did he himself possess these qualities, but he recognized that my team did as well. We were all doing it the same way. The momentum was growing and the Perfect Plan study was the forum we needed.

So, with the help of a couple of awesome interns, Mary Margret Lee and Elizabeth Beck, we started what we thought was a simple summer MNE (Multi National Enterprise) paper. It turned into, however, the first glimpse of a mystery we never knew existed, but it also gave us the key to solving the puzzle.

It forced our paths to cross with the evidence we needed to justify our reasoning, thus proving the hypothesis.

The girls spent the summer building databases on India's buying culture, while I spent the summer serving, writing papers, and designing institutional financial plans. In my spare time, I was reading and interpreting the data. I also enjoyed a few international trips that allowed for the exploration of, and working alongside, some of the world's best and brightest servants. It was exciting and full of the richest debates I have ever experienced. From market commentary in Europe to my concerns over a slower-than-expected middle class growth in China, we covered it all. Once the ladies had finished their work and I injected my thoughts, we presented it to Tim and his team of senior-level advisors. From there, it was off to the races, and the search for the Perfect Plan hit light speed.

We first began testing the Perfect Plan in Monterey, Mexico, and Mexico City, where we were exposed to some of the finest marketing and sales people I had ever met. They didn't know it at the time, but they were to become our first test subjects that would ultimately lead us to discover the process. Our study soon went global with projects in Europe, Russia, India, Australia, China, Japan, and South America.

By the summer of that second year, we were already leading the nation and possibly the industry in domestic sales, but by the time we were done with our experiments, we weren't just leading, we had lapped the field. New goals were crushed only two months into each annual cycle, and the company had to rethink their definition of the term "capacity."

The Perfect Plan came to prove that capacity was a self-induced mindset and sales goals were meaningless.

With the Perfect Plan in place, we set and broke more records faster than management could log them in their books and budgets.

The hypothesis was proven, and we had successfully induced it upon our team. Best of all, we survived and found ourselves wanting more. This was something greater than the short-term output that comes from a quick burst of focused and driven work. We thrived on it, and better yet, we never lost energy and never stopped to catch our breath — we did not need to.

The process and the Plan were so perfect that we actually created energy and desire from within.

It was here where we came to realize that most corporate middle managers drive toward the center of a bell curve that reflects a traditional sales training methodology. The challenge was that the textbook method has not been refreshed in over 100 years.

Keep in mind that all great ideas have detractors who don't want to see them succeed. For some, it is due to their natural resistance to change, while others see it as a challenge on their own limited success. In a few, it is a simple reflection of their own incompetence, fueled by the desire to rise to fame while preventing anyone else from rising higher than them. Sadly, this isn't an economical rise they are trying to squash, but a childish need to suppress others from growing when they themselves have stalled. It is just the way life is, and these folks have been around for thousands of years. I suspect they will be here for thousands more.

These folks are a prime example of what Dr. Laurence J. Peter and Raymond Hull formulated in their 1969 book, *The Peter Principle.* In short, everyone, given enough upward mobility, will rise to the level of his or her own incompetence — and there is plenty of *that* in the world. If you don't believe it, just look at Congress these days.

The Peter Principle happens in a lot of management decisions by those who don't want to unlock their team's full potential for fear that they will lose control over them. These people fail to become servants and fall with a tragic lack of humility.

You know this is happening, because the managers and senior executives who have risen far beyond their training and capabilities are forced to rethink the leadership of their own teams. This too is nothing new.

Before Peter and Hull's revelation on the subject, a similar experience was described as early as 1767 by Gotthold Ephraim Lessing in his comedy, *Minna von Barnhelm*. When translated from German to English, it tells of his own conclusions regarding his rise to leadership: "To become more than a sergeant? I don't consider it. I am a good sergeant; I might easily make a bad captain, and certainly a worse general. People have had this experience."

It is a principle that, like the Perfect Plan, spans the ages and is true and relevant in any era. To truly succeed and feel the powerful results unlocked within the Perfect Plan, there needs to be an environment committed to success of everyone on the team. No egos or fear, just sincere desire to see others grow to their fullest potential, even if it might seem greater than one's own.

We knew about this concept, and we were aware of some outside resistance building to the Perfect Plan, but it only became evident a few years later. After years of study, billions of dollars in record-breaking sales, and millions of miles traveled, I had decided to leave MetLife. It was then and has been to this day the single most difficult professional decision of my career. To leave a firm that I admired so much, and one whose leadership was so committed to everyone's success, was questioned by everyone I knew both personally and professionally. I had a simple reason for leaving, and as I had mentioned before, I don't believe in coincidences. My decision to leave was not a reflection on MetLife's leadership at all. In fact, I miss working with them every day, and who wouldn't? From Tim Mitchell and Rob Henrikson to other legendary greats like Bill Topetta, Brian Fox, George Castineiras, John Morabitto, Joe Jordan and the late Bob BenMoche, I have enjoyed working with and miss working with these dynamic and passionate individuals who only ever offered their best to everyone on their teams.

I was standing in the town square of old Prague in the Czech Republic when I felt that I was called to a new organization. One that, at the time, had similar leadership, values and desires as MetLife. It was a great organization that wanted growth but would soon find itself adrift and caught in a classic Peter Principle rift. As a result of retirements and organizational changes, a new management team intruded in such a way as to lead them to forget their passions and allowed egos to interfere. They were stalling, and it was into this meltdown that I felt compelled to jump. While there were times when I questioned the reasons I was drawn there, I soon realized that for a hypothesis and project as life-altering as the Perfect Plan to grow, it must first be tested. It tested it there.

Win the Lobster

Even though the climate quickly grew stale and the changes occurring at the new firm were uncomfortable, I had the pleasure of briefly working alongside one of the greatest managers of people I have ever met, George Sutherland.

George was the type of guy that everyone needs to know and welcome as a leader. He was a combination friend, therapist, and motivator while exuding Yoda-like wisdom and mentorship. He had been to a few rodeos in his career and was 100% committed to putting others ahead of himself. He followed each of the Perfect Plan principles before he even knew they existed. He would become our greatest test subject, and he willingly gave his time and talent without any expectation of anything in return. George was the best because he wanted everyone to outgrow him. He felt that the more mini-Yodas he could reproduce, the better the world would become, and he was right!

Under George's influence, I quickly came to realize that once the Perfect Plan was in place, all we had to do was spread the word. I knew what it was capable of doing. We just had to implement it, and once we did, our teams once again became successful beyond anyone's wildest dreams.

The impact was felt on so many levels. At first, we showed results faster than anyone in the U.S. market thought possible as we drove sales to exceed the $1 billion mark once again. That was just the beginning. Soon the real test came, and we pushed things to the brink as a team and as individuals.

The first live test came at a sales training conference in Charlotte that would become famous and infamous at the same time. It was harmless and lots of fun, but looking back, I came to realize the significance of the thought processes that were revealed by the other teams. It was a glimpse into the future.

We were sent to Charlotte to learn and train under an outside sales consultant I quickly began to appreciate and admire. He was not the typical trainer who asked you to recite the ABCs of sales (Always Be Closing). Instead, he looked at the world though a different light. He was more concerned about how you looked to a buyer and the technical impact of your "style" on the decision- makers than he was about what it was that you were selling. He put us through two days of interactive sessions and even filmed the way we stood, talked and moved in front of our buyers. It was obvious that the next few days would be enlightening and a bit exciting.

On the last day, he let us know that we would be divided into teams to role-play our presentation skills in front of our management team, whose members had flown into town to witness the results. He would supply the topic, and we had to present and hypothetically sell to the management team, who would play the part of a buying committee. To motivate us, he made it into a competition. Every team would make a presentation in front of the judges who would adjust their "character" as they saw fit in order to push us to the brink of our skill sets. The judges would then decide upon a winner, and that's where the fun began. However, it soon became brutally honest that the winning team would be held in great admiration and all others would be referred to simply as "losers."

The winning team would be judged on their skills and what they had learned from the previous day's efforts. The winning team would also be awarded a special prize. The "best of the best" would receive a pair of live Maine lobsters sent to their home. They would also get all the matching compliments of a fine lobster dinner, including clam chowder, fresh corn and even a Boston cream pie.

Oh, yes, this would be fun.

The problem was that the management team they sent was partially made up of the same executives responsible for turning the company's culture upside down in ego-driven self-destruction. Each had technically risen in the ranks to the level of their incompetence and they wanted to judge us … the creative guys.

I quickly realized that this was not going to be fun.

At the time, the task seemed simple enough for my team and me.

Win the lobsters!

Little did we know that the judges brought in from our HQ had another plan in mind. They wanted to see if our team could survive once we were separated, so they forced a new group of team members on me who were as far from being trained in the art of the Perfect Plan as anyone could get. They were really nice people, but their skill sets were based on classical techniques and, even worse, trained by a management team who must have been Larry Peter's original test group. They maximized the Peter Principle in every possible way — even to the point of wanting to compromise everyone else's successes in order to feed their own egos. It was beginning to look like a long day.

As we broke up into our new teams, we were given our assignment, which included the topic and the order in which we would be presenting. Our assignment was silly in its predictability because we drew a very difficult institutional type of sale. The only hint at any good news was that we drew the longest stick and were awarded the very last slot to present.

The corporate newbies assigned to my team thought our drawn lot was great, but I knew we had been set up. The judges wanted us to present last so we would be in front of the *entire* class, along with a host of other dignitaries they had brought to the meeting. It was, in essence, equivalent to a public hanging spectacle, but they underestimated us. They had given me enough time to whip them into shape, so to speak — 15 minutes, to be exact.

As I sat down with the team to guide and direct them to success, it became apparent how tough they wanted to make it on us. Like a fountain, they spouted out countless regimens of textbook sales steps that would have been revolutionary only in the Dark Ages. They wanted to "probe" the client—a concept I find terrifying — and then create a "disturbance" with the client's current situation so the said client could be "motivated" to buy … ouch. It was quickly clear that I needed to take control and put things into perspective. In the end, the only thing their methodology would create is a new nametag that read "loser."

I quickly took over by asking them about our goals, and I was shocked at their answers. Each wanted to actually present a sale to this hypothetical Board of Directors and to follow predefined steps in closing the deal. They were eager and excited, but unfortunately, they were also being led by their own leadership to the slaughter.

I listened to them the best I could and even took notes in order to appear engaged, but it came to the point where I had to step in and stop the nonsense. I asked them a few simple questions and was satisfied that they were willing to take direction. I asked them to describe how they as a team were motivated to "nudge" the client to select us as the product of choice. They were speechless. My question didn't follow their preprogrammed set of steps. To get them on track with the Perfect Plan, I needed to get them off track first. In other words, I needed to reprogram the way they thought about their thinking.

So I asked another simple question, "What do you personally want to achieve in this exercise?" No one seemed to know, so I gave them the answer, "I want to win the lobsters!" Yes, win the lobsters. In fact, not only should they be motivated to win the lobsters, but they should want to win it by the largest margin in the competition's history. They should be prepared to celebrate like there is no tomorrow when they get home and find the lobsters on their doorsteps. Success in this case was not about following a technical path — we certainly could not sell anything to a hypothetical board or improperly motivated set of buyers — but we could win the lobsters. That was what this was really all about. They quickly became motivated.

They then spent the next seven minutes (the rest of our prep time) receiving the world's fastest crash course on the Perfect Plan. I convinced them that if they followed the simple steps I had outlined for them, our odds of winning were better than they could imagine. All sat on the edge of their seats, took notes and opened their minds like the professionals they would soon grow to become. This handpicked, mid-level team of Peter Principle poster children had begun a process that would not only plant the seeds of change in their own lives, but the seeds of their future and the incredibly successful careers they would come to enjoy.

For the first time, I began to see what would happen when the Perfect Plan was tested in adversity. I knew that I had been set up to fail by a group of middle managers that would judge by perception and would rather see others fail than grow. I jumped for joy when I saw what was beginning to happen. My little team of underdogs began to reverse their own paths, opening their minds to a new idea they found to be revolutionary. In less than 10 minutes, they were exposed to the Perfect Plan and clearly focused on the goal of winning the lobsters. They trusted me, and we walked into the room ready for victory.

I was thrilled to see their actions that afternoon. They were flawless in delivering their presentation, and they followed the Perfect Plan with elite precision. We were so good that not only did we avoid our own hanging, but the same judges who had set us up to fail gave us a perfect score. The proctor told us later that it was the first perfect score he had ever seen in his 20-plus year career! The team was exceptional.

The Perfect Plan had worked when tested, true, but it had done much more than that. It had elevated our team members to a level that I hoped would continue indefinitely.

The Perfect Plan won, and it had won big.

It was not just the lobsters that defined us that day; it was the test against adversity that caused the victory note to sound so clear. I know the win that day was nothing compared to similar victories the Plan had achieved in the past, but the triumph was huge and the proof undeniable.

The Perfect Plan would be tested several times again, and before long, another change was in store for me. This time, it was a change of celebration, and it seemed like everything was heading to where it was always meant to be. It was going home, and the original "radical" hypothesis was proven true, even if it was never part of the goal.

So, there it was ... a story that began with a simple idea.

It was proven by a test, ridiculed by a trial, and survived on its truth.

It not only survived, it grew beyond all expectations. The proof was clear with billions of dollars in sales, growth more than anyone had ever dreamed possible, and a team of future leaders who would help change the world.

In the end, it is a message that would help others in ways we never could envision.

It was *perfect*.

A Few Who Make Up the Elite 1%

Every year, we try to recognize the companies and individuals who are not only in the 1% club but best represent the six core principles of the Perfect Plan. This is not for those who have endorsed the Perfect Plan, but a chance for us to endorse them. They are the best of the best and live to *serve*.

Some honorees were in the original test groups and others are discovered through random acts and long-term relations. Either way, they are the best, and we want to recognize them for their work — not just today, but every day and for every life they touch.

Standouts

- ❖ Ritz Carlton
- ❖ Chick-fil-A
- ❖ Dana Barrett
- ❖ James Laschinger
- ❖ David Griffin
- ❖ North Point Ministries
- ❖ Triumph Motorcycles
- ❖ Brian Fox - MetLife
- ❖ U.S. Army Rangers
- ❖ JonPaul's
- ❖ Clark Howard
- ❖ American Century Investments
- ❖ OneAmerica Financial Partners
- ❖ 3Ci

Exemplifying the Principle of Gratification

Ritz Carlton – "It's my pleasure."

Not many in today's world can openly express their heartfelt desire to serve others better than the folks at the Ritz Carlton. Their five-star hotels represent 100 years of exemplary service, which is focused solely on their guests. Their motto says it all: "We are Ladies and Gentlemen serving Ladies and Gentlemen." One of the most outward acts of gratification occurs when Ritz Carlton employees receive a simple "thank you" from a guest. When they reply, it is never with the customary, "You're welcome," but with their signature statement, "It's my pleasure."

At the Ritz Carlton, they realize that it is a pleasure to serve others and they are not afraid to say it, or believe it. Their simple act of gratification sets them apart like no other. When people ask what it takes to be in the Top 1%, it's easy to direct them to the Ritz Carlton way of doing business and its foundational belief that serving others is not an act or deed, it is a pleasure.

Chick-fil-A – Every Life Has a Story

In 1946, when the late Truett Cathy opened his first restaurant, he had one thing in mind and, oddly enough, it was not about fast food but "quick service." He also set the tone by deciding not to be open on Sundays. It was, in their words, as much of a practical decision as it was spiritual. Truett always wanted to thank his employees by giving them a day to rest. This allows them to spend time with family and friends as well as worship where they please. By showing this level of gratitude for over 70 years, Chick-fil-A has become one of the world's leading restaurants, and their corporate giving is in a field all to itself.

While great business management and good decisions continue to lead the company to become a great powerhouse in their market, it is really about their service to others and the way they see the world. A few years ago, one of the greatest training videos of all-time hit the social media world and allowed the outside to glimpse into the wonderful and grateful world of a Chick-fil-A employee. If you want to see what real acts of gratification are in today's world, search for the video, and you will be amazed and humbled: *Every Life Has a Story*. It will change the way you see the world, and allow you experience why they understand gratification and service.

Exemplifying the Principle of Education

Dana Barrett – Do the Right Thing

Looking around the world for the Elite 1% taught us that it is not a mechanical scale or a meter that declares someone worthy, but a way of being. It is the core of who you are as a person and how you approach others. It is about servant leadership and using the unique path of your own life to impact others. To me, there is no better example than that of TV and radio personality Dana Barrett.

For millions of people every weekday morning, Dana's voice welcomes them into a new day with real-life global business commentary that is sprinkled with local focus. With the power of a morning drive-time radio show on the Wall Street Business Network, she delivers honest insight into the world around her and is never afraid to say, or do, the right thing. Most importantly, she is kind and compassionate to everyone she highlights on her show, as she allows him or her to springboard off her celebrity platform to help grow their own.

As kind as she is to those who serve others, Dana is not afraid to call out business leaders who take advantage of people in her always-anticipated annual year-end video report, "The Top Lying Liars." In her commentary, she looks back over the previous 12 months to revisit those who lied, cheated, and stole their way to the top, all while riding on the backs of those who they purportedly served. She is fearless in her attempts to hold others accountable and reminds her listeners to seek the best because nothing short will do.

Dana is the example of servant leadership everyone should model. She has taken her unique ability to communicate, motivate and inspire and combined it with academic excellence. From hosting TEDx Events, to her countless commitments to charity and local needs, she does everything in her power to highlight the good we see around us. Best of all, she leads the way and always does the right thing for everyone she meets.

James Laschinger – Where a Dashboard First Found a Boardroom

What happens when a tennis prodigy and NCAA Champion meets Wall Street? He builds a Dashboard, of course.

James Laschinger, or J, as he is known, was built for athletic success, but few saw the future as well as he did — and still does today. "I knew that my ability to play tennis at the University of Georgia would afford me the education I would need to serve others." It was just a matter of time before the NCAA Arthur Ashe Award winner would make his mark off the court and stamp it on Wall Street.

J has always known that people are auditory, and in many cases, they understand what is being told to them better than what they can read for themselves. This is what led J to create one of the first financial dashboards. "I wanted to help my clients make educated decisions about very complex issues without requiring them to become the expert, because that's why they hire me."

J is always the first to give credit to his clients, but also delivers educational excellence at a level that impresses even others in the Elite 1%. As one of the original test subjects, J opened his practice to us and brought us into a world where sports and Wall Street met in a way that allowed everyone to participate. "I work hard to create reports that are so simple to read. Everyone walks away having made a good decision and the ability to justify their vote. I want to be the one who delivers their 'good news.' "

J's clients are some of the most recognized brands in the world, and all appreciate his ability to educate them in a way they can maintain focus without being caught in the massive amounts of detail.

"I want them to run their business and not have to worry about the daily in and out movements of the stock markets. I also want them to understand and be informed. That is why I created the Dashboard … now everyone can make wise decisions."

J took his championship mindset to the world, but he is not focused on winning it for himself. "I want to help others be champions as well."

By serving others with education, J teaches everyone that you hold a trophy the highest when it is held for others.

Exemplifying the Principle of Ease of Business

David Griffin – CS001

David Griffin holds a special place in Perfect Plan history by being tagged CS001, or Case Study #1. We were first magnetized to David when he was a recent college graduate, making his way into the corporate world. We met with David by accident, but we instantly knew he was wired to be different. His genuine charm and desire to serve others was coupled with a personality that resembled the fictional persona in the wonderful Dos Equis advertising campaign, "The Most Interesting Man in the World." Only he had achieved it years before the famous commercial had aired.

David, even at an early age, had a simple philosophy that separated him from the others. He believes service makes people's lives easier by freeing them with the truth.

"I believe people don't need more work or crisis in their lives, they are actually seeking an easier place to live and work, so that's why they hire me." David goes on to explain that the best way to make anyone's life better is by helping him or her find the truth. To ease someone's burden, you have to discover the reason for their distraction before you can set them on a course to freedom. That process involves creating an environment that is safe and inviting. He always welcomes people with open arms and solves their problems in a way that puts people at ease. "I never want to expose an issue with negative or painful emotions. People have enough of that in their lives without bringing it to their work," he said. "I focus on making their lives easier by helping them understand that we can work together to make complex issues simple so their lives will be at peace."

North Point Ministries – If It Looks Easy, It's Not

What is Andy Stanley's and North Point Ministries' secret to serving over 30,000 people every Sunday? Make it look easy!

In 1995, a vision was set forth that changed the way the modern church came to look, feel and, most importantly, *serve*. It revolved around an idea focused on creating an environment where everyone, even those who never attended a church before, would love to go and spend time. This ultimately became the foundation upon which tens of thousands came to attend a weekly event. Services tend to have the same casual feel as attending a play or a movie. You never have to worry about being judged or live a certain way. That's when the magic happens!

As the weekly program begins, everyone feels compelled to participate in a way that works best for him or her. The audience environment is similar to doing a wave at a football game; it is fun, exciting, and everyone can do it. Before long, you find yourself enjoying some of the world's elite musicians, singing songs ranging from the Beatles to ESPN's Sports Center theme. Nothing is out of reach when it comes to creating the world's most magnetizing environment for everyone to enjoy.

Though it may look easy, it is not.

Every week, hundreds of employees and volunteers come together to make your experience so easy and relaxed that you never notice the sheer volume of people, cars, and logistics necessary to move 30,000 people in and out of a location with a one-hour turnaround.

The focus and energy that goes into making every attendees experience "easy" is nothing short of miraculous. From the parking lot attendants and greeters to their state-of-the-art technology and video, the attendees are totally relaxed as they experience one of the greatest speakers in history, Andy Stanley, deliver a message of hope and love to people here, there, and everywhere.

Best of all, it is easy ... for you, that is.

Exemplifying the Principle of Create – Don't Compete

Triumph Motorcycles – Where "Cool" Meets the Elite 1%

As the Perfect Plan study took our teams around the world, it became apparent that the Elite 1% rarely found fame outside their nucleus of work. In fact, most of the subjects were rarely known outside of their immediate environment or those whom they served, but that was not true for this company. As we came to know Triumph Motorcycles and their work, it became apparent that they were not only building some of the world's best motorcycles, they were also building a culture.

For over 100 years, the U.K. brand of Triumph Motorcycles has been associated with a lifestyle that surpasses their product and the competition. When we began to study their phenomenon, we realized they were much more than a product; their creativity was impacting a culture.

While there are certainly other great brands in the motorcycle world, we discovered something special happened when anyone would mention the name "Triumph." The response was always the same: "Cool."

When we tested this unusual response, we quickly discovered why their incredible magnetism worked.

Steve McQueen, Fonzie, Marlon Brando in *The Wild Ones*, Ann Margaret, Angelina Jolie, Harrison Ford, the Matrix movie characters, Clint Eastwood, and even Elvis — all iconic figures in culture have one thing in common. They rode Triumph Motorcycles.

In the process of creating and building one of the world's finest products, Triumph decided not to compete with other manufacturers, but to create an icon for the ages. In doing so, they secured themselves in the Elite 1% club by focusing on a magnetism that transformed multiple generations while remaining timeless in their spirit. That's cool.

MetLife and **Brian Fox** – Life at its Best

MetLife is without question one of the largest firms represented on the Perfect Plan's list of the Elite 1%, and that makes it all the more special.

One of the primary indicators we discovered that prevented several companies from moving into the Elite 1% was their size. In many cases, a company's size becomes so cumbersome that it's like trying to control a teenage dinosaur — the desire is there, but asking something of such proportion to change directions and focus is an entirely different thing. Thankfully for MetLife and their Chief Marketing Officer, Brian Fox, that is not the case for one of America's most distinguished and historical firms.

In 1908, MetLife built the tallest building in the world, causing reporters to write that is was literally "scraping the sky." When completed, MetLife placed a light on top of the building for the entire world to see, but little did they realize how impactful that light would become. The building went on to serve history in more ways than anyone could have imagined. From housing the survivors of the Titanic, to becoming the nation's largest buyer of bonds during WWII, MetLife began creating opportunities for America that spanned beyond typical insurance and became a synergy for creativity that would change the world.

As the largest backer of American farm mortgages during the Great Depression to the first to use computers in the 1950s, MetLife consistently found ways to create opportunities while never focusing on their competitors.

"We have always sought to do the right thing and create solutions beyond our product offerings" says Brian Fox, CMO and a member of the Elite 1% club himself.

"While we absolutely *love* our relationship with the famous Peanuts characters, we also enjoy impacting people's lives around the globe in ways few might ever know."

One such moment happened on a crisp fall September day in 2001.

"September 11th was a dark day for us at MetLife," said Fox. "We lost a lot of great people that morning, and their legacy will be with us forever."

As anyone who has ever seen a picture of New York City knows, MetLife is a fixture in the city's skyline, towering above Grand

Central Station with a marquee for everyone to see. As open as they are about their presence in NYC, few people get to go inside the hearts and minds of the senior management teams at MetLife. If so, you might understand their desire to create a new beginning that day in 2001, for the city and ultimately America.

"It was never a hard decision for us to do the right thing," explained Brian. "Our CEO at the time never hesitated as we immediately began pumping money back into the U.S. economy by flushing $1 billion in cash back into the U.S. stock markets to help shore up our economy crippled by the attacks."

MetLife also did something no one would have ever guessed, as Brian tells with a warm and enduring smile, "We immediately began paying life insurance claims for the victims of the attacks; we never hesitated."

The wonderful thing about this act is that they never required death certificates or any real proof that the victims were lost. They simply paid the claims.

"MetLife has always done the right thing, and we always will. It is built into our heritage and the core belief of our people to serve others and create opportunities from our vast resources that go far beyond products, investments, and properties."

Some of MetLife's success is their belief that being the best means never having "hobbies." As Brian and others likes to say, "If we don't believe we can be #1 or #2 in a particular market space, there is no need to try, because we are not in the 'hobby' business, but in the service business."

Brian said, "We serve by being the best we can be, which allows us to unleash our creativity and in turn provide resources, capital, and aid when people need it most."

Brian is a third-generation MetLife employee and loves every second of it.

"I wake up every day and run to my office," he said with unbridled enthusiasm. "Where else can I live in such a creative environment serving others, while surrounded with the world's best and brightest minds all focused on being the best you can be? What a blessing!"

Brian has been one of the Elite 1% for a long time, and his work within MetLife guarantees MetLife's status in the same category for years to come.

Exemplifying the Principle of the Value is Greater than the Cost

U.S. Army Rangers – Rangers Lead the Way

When our study began, seeking to discover the secrets to the world's best in leadership, sales and marketing, we never thought it would lead us to the U.S. Army's 1st and 3rd Ranger Battalions, 75th Regiment stationed at Ft. Benning and Hunter Army Air Field in Columbus and Savannah Georgia. Little did we know the Rangers would quickly become the story behind the real meaning of the Perfect Plan.

The U.S. Army Rangers' history dates back to the 17th century, but they were first organized during the American Revolutionary War. They have fought to defend the world's freedom for over 200 years and continue representing the bravest among us today. While we never thought to study them in the beginning, they won the unanimous vote as the best in this particular principle without anyone having to question or ask why.

While spending time among their ranks and leadership, we discovered they epitomize the concept of a value being greater than the price. In their situation, the "price" is more than what most people would ever be willing to pay.

"Every day, there is a Ranger deployed in harm's way, sleeping in the mud, putting his life on the line thousands of miles from home. They do this willingly so you can live in peace," said Richard Schooley, one of the founders of the Sua Sponte Foundation, the Rangers support charity based in Savannah, Georgia.

"We live to serve them, knowing they are volunteering to serve us, making the ultimate sacrifice every day," said their biggest supporter, David Ermer.

The U.S. Army Rangers are an elite group of soldiers.

As with all men and women in military service, they seek to exceed expectations and *give forward* with a commitment few people can understand.

As it is written at the Ranger Memorial in Savannah, from John 15:13:

Greater love has no one than this:
to lay down one's life for one's friends.

RLTW

JonPaul's – European Tradition Comes to America

A few years ago, a famous American credit card company ran an ad campaign entitled "priceless." It focused on the times in your life where you look back and realize the moment had a value that exceeded life's expectation. The commercials implied that these moments were few and far between, so you had better be ready. Fortunately for the rest of the world, someone already had a better idea.

Dr. JonPaul Leskie received his Ph.D. in computer science from the University of California before he spent a few years at MIT working on some really cool stuff. He touched everything from the world's leading telecommunication companies to homeland security. Thankfully for the world, JonPaul is a good guy, and better yet, as one of the world's Elite 1%, he thinks a little out of the box.

"Why should you have to wait for those priceless moments in life?" he said. "Why not just make it happen?"

The idea came to him one day in Europe when he went to get a haircut and experienced something magical. His experience prompted him to ask, "What would a man pay if he could purposely schedule time to step away from the world?"

"What is we could create a place where they could come in perfect peace, even if only for an hour every other week, to recharge, relax, and be served by the world's best professionals?"

He knew the social buyers pyramid (chapter 4), recognizing time and the return on investment, was the key driver for decisions among the C Suite, so he created the ultimate experience with a value greatly exceeding the price.

Everyone gets a haircut these days, and conveniently enough, his wife Cathy is not only a master barber but also one of the world's unique personalities.

"It really is the 'Cathy Show' here at JonPaul's," he said. It is where a gentleman can come for an hour and a half to experience true relaxation with a traditional haircut, shave, facial, shoulder massage, shoe shine, and even a cocktail. Time stands still for these guys while they relax and experience a little of Cathy's worldly wisdom and therapy.

"I always treat the guys right, and I am so appreciative when they ask for my advice on things they can't ask their peers or co-workers about their business," she says.

"CEOs and business owners are a lonely group, and if I can be here to help and lend a bit of wisdom, I am all for it," she says, "Running this business is no different from any other, so I can relate and offer them a moment of relaxing service while they bounce ideas around, feeling great about their appearance when they leave."

Cathy has staffed the firm with elite, like-minded professionals in men's grooming. From deep-tissue sports massages to April's manicures, everything is offered from cigars to custom suites, accessories to styling products. It's a one-stop shop for the guy who wants to step away for a moment and be served in a way they deserve before they walk back into the world and face tomorrow's challenges.

"The best part of JonPaul's," said frequent customer Dr. Burke Robinson, "is the value-to-price ratio."

"I am always amazed, when I slip into such a wonderful place and feel like I have been treated like a king!" said retired CEO and Harvard Business School graduate Fred Erler.

Even better, JonPaul's is for everyone. You don't have to be a CEO, Ph.D., M.D., or business owner to appreciate the ultimate value and experience. JonPaul's is designed for everyone and has succeeded in creating a priceless moment that, for once, can be scheduled and repeated at will.

Clark Howard – The Clark Howard Show

Clark is one of the top radio and TV personalities in the world today, and that's pretty special for such a regular guy. One of the reasons Clark was chosen as a stand out among the Elite 1% was his connection with people and his acceptance of a unique responsibility. Clark understands that 85% of a decision is based on emotion and then justified with 15% of the facts, so he set out to help people with the "justification" portion of the formula.

"I want to help people save money," says Clark every day on his nationally syndicated radio show. "We are here to serve, and help people find the best deals and avoid getting ripped off."

Best of all, Clark's services are free to everyone.

Whether you watched him on CNN's Headline News, visited his website, or listen to him on any of 200-plus radio stations that broadcast his show daily, you quickly discover that Clark is the real thing.

Clark gives advice to anyone who wants to understand value. Not only has he published over nine books on his favorite subjects, he offers free advice off the air through 145-plus volunteers all dedicated to serving others.

We first met Clark officially a few years ago, when he accepted a last-minute invitation to speak at a   high school graduation in Atlanta. The original speaker cancelled at the last moment, leaving the school with little hope to fill the slot. After a few calls and a local family connection, Clark jumped at the chance to fill in, but there was a little snag.

Clark's fee at the time for speaking at private events was $15,000 an hour. While many find that expensive, those who know Clark and his message realize that that is a check well worth writing. What makes Clark extra special is when people discover to whom you write the check if you want to hear Clark speak at your event. You never write the check to Clark, but directly to Habitat for Humanity.

Wow!

A guy who can command $15,000 an hour does not accept the money but asks that you give it forward to one of his favorite charities so you can help others have a place to call home.

Wow again!

When the high school heard about the fee, they were a worried at first but made it work. Clark graciously told them not to worry about the full $15,000 but to do what they could.

This incredible act of kindness created a lesson in life for the kids, who were so motivated by Clark that they volunteered to work all summer raising enough money to build a Habitat for Humanity home themselves. Clark taught them more than grace. He motivated them to serve others as well.

Wow again and again, but there is more …

Clark was so moved by what these kids had agreed to do, he took one more step toward serving others in a way no one expected. While on stage and graciously hearing what the kids had announced they would accomplish for others, Clark raised the bar as only he could.

Visibly moved by the kids' kind act to volunteer building a Habitat House, Clark announced that he would match their generosity dollar-for-dollar and build a second Habitat for Humanity house alongside theirs (with his own money) in order to make the gift twice as impactful to families in need.

Wow, wow, wow indeed.

By helping others justify value and save money, Clark teaches us how to best use our resources to serve others.

One of the students was overheard saying something that summer that summed it all up: "The money you save is worthless unless you help others and make the world a better place."

They are right, and Clark's education continues to impact others well beyond their bank account.

Exemplifying the Principle of Giving Forward

American Century Investments – Profits with a Purpose

Being based in Kansas City may help explain why one of Wall Street's best-known brands is one of the country's most forward-giving and benevolent organizations. With a relatively simple understanding that they are from Main Street, not Wall Street, they focus on their customer first by helping them get to a better place.

Since 1958, American Century has managed billions of dollars for their customers with a promise to always do the right thing, but it goes much deeper.

"American Century Investments is guided by core values that shape the way we conduct our business. These have been in place since 1958, when James E. Stowers Jr. founded the company, and they have not changed," says long-time employee Bruce Caldwell.

"These values include a strong commitment to helping others and building a strong community".

In 1994, Jim and Virginia Stowers, the company's founders, decided they wanted to give back something "more valuable than money" to the millions of people who helped make their success possible.

As cancer survivors, Jim and Virginia decided to focus on a way to improve the quality of others' lives so they, too, could survive. That is when they decided to create the **Stowers Institute for Medical Research,** one of the most innovative biomedical research organizations in the world.

American Century to this day lives out the Stowers' model of giving something "more valuable than money." They strategically focus by *giving forward* more than 40% of their profits to support research to help cure genetically-based diseases, including cancer, diabetes, and dementia.

Today, their leadership is driven more than ever to give forward, understanding their existence helps folks beyond the product lines. CEO Jonathan Thomas is a passionate supporter of their mission: *Profits with a Purpose.*

Jonathan works tirelessly to promote the company's mission to help others find the hope of one day living cancer-free. Their commitment is monumental and they forge ahead every day with a mission to help others survive. Surrounded with an elite executive team and a clear plan, they hope to exceed their client's expectations, but also change the world.

OneAmerica Financial Partners – Bigger Is Not Better; Better Is Better

When OneAmerica's legendary retired CEO Dayton Molendorp first uttered the words, "Bigger is not better; better is better," it stuck.

With a commitment to be there when their clients need them most, the OneAmerica family of firms has built their 150-plus year history on a culture of service, fueled by a "servant's heart."

"We are big enough to matter, but small enough to care," said Bill Yoerger, the company's past President and Divisional head.

"We grow through hard work and commitment, but we never forget why," said senior executive Mark Glavin. "We are here to serve."

There seem to be countless examples of the company's commitment to give forward, from Mark Wilkerson's "Run Mark Run" campaign to feed children in Haiti, to the endless dedication of their employees to support their local community. None shines as bright as when the company meets for its annual meetings.

As a group who encourages and supports every employee to give forward as individuals, few companies can say that they volunteer an entire work day to help feed the world. In the summer of 2011, in Colorado Springs, over 300 OneAmerica employees gave up a day of their vacation time to help support and feed over 100,000 people creating meals for the Kids Around the World program.

"OneAmerica knows there are many organizations that claim to be in the financial services field, but those folks are usually in the financial processing business," explained Mark Glavin. "At OneAmerica, we are in the 'financial services' business because we are servants and that says it all."

Dayton Molendorp once said, "When someone shows you who they really are, believe them."

With OneAmerica, it is easy to know who they are, and easy to believe them. They are Servants, who serve others by giving forward with a promise that they will always be there when you need them most.

3Ci – Where Technology Has a Heart

124

The 3Ci story started one fateful day in the mid-1970s when Pat McBrayer, a respected IT consultant, became fed up with the way things worked. Troubled by the unethical business practices he witnessed in the emerging IT industry, including his own résumé being misrepresented to a client without his knowledge, Pat decided there had to be a better way, so he went out on his own, and the rest, as they say, is history.

Pat and his wife, Charleen, were among the pioneers in the IT professional services industry when they launched a one-customer consulting business in Atlanta called Comprehensive Computer Consulting, Inc. First incorporated in 1978, five decades later, their first customer is still a 3Ci client today. Pat and Charleen grew 3Ci from a company with one IT consultant to a thriving firm that today employs more than 400 IT professionals and serves a diverse and prestigious client base.

But that is just the beginning.

Putting people first is what they are all about, and it is the reason for 40 years of success.

Since day one, 3Ci seemed to march to a different drummer, placing the value of people and relationships above all else. Their dedication to building the business one relationship at a time and putting people first has survived the test of time and propelled 3Ci's growth through even the most challenging economic times.

Upon Pat's tragic passing in 1995, Charleen became CEO and held firm to Pat's vision of helping IT professionals and connecting customers with high-quality technology services. "I remember when it struck me after Pat's death that we not only had several hundred employees, but we had several hundred families," said Charleen. "I was not about to let them down."

Guided by 3Ci's principles and values, Charleen took the reins and steadily grew the business into the premier IT professional services firm it is today, but in addition to hard work, Charleen and her team focus on the most precious principle of all, Giving Forward.

Every day, somewhere around the world, a 3Ci employee is giving forward to their community, clients, and family. Whether it is a Donate Life Campaign for organ donors, participating in the Transplant Games, or washing kids' feet and giving them new shoes through Samaritan's Feet, 3CI is there, and they are serving with a passion.

"It is why we are here," said 3Ci President Rob MacLane, "to serve others and hopefully support and provide them a better life." He went on to say, "Technology is a skill where we excel better than most, but it is not our purpose. We are here to serve people – clients, communities and families. It is just who we are."

3Ci has supplied over 10,000,000 hours of IT staff support, but that does not compare to the number of lives they have impacted across the globe. That's what makes them special and a leader within the world's Elite 1%. Giving forward is not just an action, it is a life. It is who you are, and no one does it with the heart and soul of 3Ci.

In 2014, The Perfect Plan and 3Ci combined to share with the world that technology really does have a heart.

Here's to another 40 years of serving others.

Jeremiah 29:11
New International Version

"For I know the plans I have for you," says the Lord. "Plans to prosper you and not harm you, plans to give you hope and a future".

About the Author:

Donald W. Barden

To many, Don Barden is a classically trained economist who is fluent in international business affairs, but as he likes to say, "I am really a frustrated anthropologist!" Even though he loves to lecture and teach on world affairs and the economy, he is always quick to point out that he cares more about "why people make decisions," than he does about "yield curves and interest rates."

Don loves motivating people to think deeply about their beliefs. His "unfair advantage" theories are revolutionary in today's world. Don will lead you on a journey that exposes the myth of modern leadership, sales and marketing as he identifies the pathway to consistent cultural change.

Expertly mixing humor and academic capital, Don engages audiences through his highly personal and interactive writing and speaking style. Don will shake your fundamental belief systems and reset your foundations with his unique ability to break down barriers and build an irresistible and motivated force that is focused on growth and the future.

As an author, speaker, advisor and business owner, Don Barden offers counsel that is highly sought after by some of the world's most successful businesses. His experience and record-setting sales success have drawn him to corporate and political leaders who want to tap into his real-world expertise in order to move their organizations to higher levels of achievement. Don has personally worked with some of the world's best-known brands and has reshaped the production landscape of three major financial institutions. He personally averaged over $1 billion a year in annual sales.

He has an M.B.A. in Global Technology Management and International Business as well as an undergraduate B.B.A. in Economics and Finance. He is also ABD with a Ph.D. in Behavioral Economics.

Don is the past Board Chairman of the Summit Counseling Center in Atlanta, a multi-disciplined facility delivering over 7,000 clinical hours of therapy per year, and he is a passionate supporter of the Sua Sponte Foundation and the 1st Ranger Battalion stationed at Hunter Airfield in Savannah, Georgia.

Special Thanks to everyone who contributed over the years...

Lisa, Jake, Luke, and Nick for your love and patience!

Kyle Lenard – The guy who made it happen.

Bruce Marciano, John Maxwell, Ravi Zacharias, Allen Hunt, David and Vicki Smith, and all of the doctors, counselors and staff at the Summit Counseling Center, for the life-changing moments

Mike Kaplan, Casey Jones III, Neal Howard, and Rick Swerdlin

Dave Bigler, John Pickard, Patrick Barry, Mike Voegele, Tom Nicol, Don Weitzel, Scott Fenstermaker, Scott Fjeldstad, Mike Robinson, and Robb Hill

Scott Keller CFA, Gene Henssler Ph.D., Ted Parrish CFA, Retired U.S. Navy Cmdr. Michael S. Quinlan

George Castineiras, C. Robert Henrikson, Robert BenMosche, William Toppeta, Tim Mitchell, Brian J Fox, Robert Merck, William Wheeler, Maria Morris, Joe Jordan, Larry Karl and John Morabito

Fred Castellani, George Sutherland, Jim Gilligan, Scott Pawlitch, Tanya Jones, Palmer Whitney, Bill Feldmeir, Shefali Desai, Sarah Elliott, and with special memories to Robert Cunningham

Dayton Molendorp, J. Scott Davidson, Mark Roller, Brian Lauber, Mark Wilkerson, Bill Yoerger, Mark Glavin, Marsha Whitehead, Angela Trefethen, Mitch Haber, Ana Etcheverry, and Eric Pete

Erin Mitchell, Lauren Maifei, Scott Brown, Alice Davis and Brittany Behn

Burke Robinson, George Norton, Fred Erler, Ron Murray, Fritz Scheffel, Anthony Walsh, Noland Deas, Kirk Somers, Jim Milar, Phillip and Robin McEuen

Indiana, Kansas, Canada, as well as the UK, Italy, Czech Republic, Germany, France, Mexico, India, Brazil, Peru, Indonesia, Costa Rica, Belize, Panama, Australia, New Zealand, China and Japan

Dan Sullivan, Kristi Chambers and the entire Strategic Coach team

Ford and Christi Smith for your art and inspiration

Greg Baker

Artist Brandon Wattenbarger

Kennesaw State University, University of Oxford (UK), Heron University (UK), Georgia State University, American InterContinental University, Walden University, University of Georgia, Auburn University

To all the test subjects, organizations, and companies around the world who let us into their lives only for us to discover that our hearts were changed by your service to us and others, we thank you.

For more information on The Perfect Plan, with updates of people and organizations that make up the Elite 1%, visit our website at:

www.theperfectplantoday.com

www.donbardenstheperfectplan.com

For blogs and videos from Don, please visit:

www.3cipeople.com

You can also follow us on Facebook, LinkedIn, Twitter and YouTube.

Don Barden can be reached at don@dwbarden.com